MILITARY AVIATION LIBRARY
Modern
United States
Aircraft

The United States Air Force

The United States Air Force is undoubtedly a most formidable military machine. Equipped with the most advanced fighters currently available, advanced early-warning aircraft equipped with "look-down" surveillance radar, a fleet of intercontinental-range jet transports capable of projecting military power across the globe, more than 200 long-range heavy bombers capable of attacking targets with free-falling bombs or the latest cruise missiles, and a land-based deterrent in the shape of more than 1,000 intercontinental missiles, it represents a military capability which no other nation can match. Whereas USAF's F-15 Eagle fighter entered service in the mid 1970s, the nearest Soviet equivalent—the MiG-29 Fulcrum—is probably only just becoming operational, and the F-16 Fighting Falcon provides the yardstick against which the performance of future Soviet air-combat fighters must be judged.

The air arm of the United States did not achieve its status as an independent service until 1947, having been a branch of the US Army until then. It started life in 1907 as the Aeronautical Division of the Signal Corps, later being renamed the Aviation Section of the Signal Corps. In 1918 it became the Army Air Service, but was elevated to the status of the Army Air Corps in 1926. The latter title was retained until 1941, when a further "promotion" introduced the title Army Air Forces. Final independence came on September 18, 1947, and the service has been known as the United States Air Force since that date.

It may be that this late transition to the status of a separate service had a detrimental influence on the procurement and operating policies in the decades which followed. Certainly, the USAF has twice adopted US Navy front-line aircraft—the F-4 Phantom and the A-7 Corsair II—while the service's "kill ratio" against North Vietnamese fighters for a long time lagged behind that of the US Navy.

Organization

Main components of the USAF are Strategic Air Command (SAC), Tactical Air Command (TAC), Military Airlift Command (MAC), Air Training Command (ATC), United States Air Forces in Europe (USAFE), Pacific Air Force (PAF), and Alaskan Air Command (AAC).

These are supported by four further Commands—Air Force Communications Command (AFCC), Air Force Logistics Command (AFLC), Air Force Systems Command (AFSC), and Electronic Security Command (ESC). Further support is given by 13 Separate Operating Agencies (SOAs), covering fields from commissary and safety to legal and counter-intelligence services, plus a number of Direct Reporting Units (DRUs) such as the Air Force Academy, Air Reserve Personnel Center and the Simpson Historical Research Center.

Like most air arms, the USAF front-line aircraft strength can vary from year to year. During the early 1980s the number showed a slight annual increase. In Fiscal Year 1983, a total of 7,305 aircraft were deployed. A further 485 were available from the Air Force Reserve, and 458 from the Air National Guard.

Most fighter or attack squadrons have either 18 or 24 aircraft. Bomber squadrons can have anything from 12 to 19 aircraft, 12 or 13 in the case of FB-111 units. Typical transport squadrons have 16 C-130 Hercules, 17 to 18 C-5A Galaxies or 18 C-141 StarLifters. Units operating specialized aircraft tend to vary in strength. An E-3A Sentry squadron for example could have between 2 and 17 aircraft.

The USAF has 94 bases in the USA, plus 43 main bases in overseas nations. The Air National Guard and Air Force Reserve operate from a total of 85 bases in the USA. Some are shared with the USAF.

Just over 80 percent of the USAF personnel ing specialized aircraft tend to vary in strength. account for 17 percent, the remainder being cadets. More than 85,000 black personnel serve with the USAF, making up some 15 percent of the enlisted manpower, and five percent of the officers. Black personnel form an above-average share of enlisted ranks such as staff sergeant, sergeant and senior airman, but are less well represented at the higher levels of command. Women play an ever-growing role in USAF strength, making up about 10 percent of the total.

Service personnel are well educated. More than 1,000 officers plus a handful of enlisted personnel have Doctoral or professional degrees, while virtually all officers have a Batchelor's or Master's degree. The later qualifications are also held by around two percent of enlisted personnel, while around 20 percent have some level of college education. Seventy-five percent of all enlisted personnel have a High School education, with only a few percent falling below this category.

Strategic Air Command

Strategic Air Command is responsible for the ground and airborne portions of the "triad" of US strategic forces. When Boeing engineers designed the B-52 bomber in the early 1950s, they could have had no idea that the aircraft would serve into the 1980s. The search for an eventual replacement has run for two decades, the Mach-3 B-70 having been cancelled in the 1960s, with the later B-1 being delayed by President Carter's decision to cancel the original program.

By the mid-1980s, the average age of USAF's B-52s will be a quarter of a century. The original projected airframe life was only 5,000 hours, a figure which even the youngest passed more than a decade ago, but a massive structural rebuild program has prolonged service life and enabled the aircraft to cope with the stresses involved in low-level flight.

The main bomber force consists of 269 B-52G and B-52H bombers (plus some sharply differing B-52Ds now being withdrawn from the active inventory). In order to improve avionics performance and to eliminate the problems associated with the maintenance of elderly vacuum-tube (thermionic valve) avionics, these aircraft are being re-equipped with modern solid-state electronics hardened to resist the effects of electro-magnetic pulses from nuclear explosions. The new avionics include a modernized radar, and new inertial navigation and bombing systems.

The USAF retains its unique position as the world's most technically advanced air arm. Its roles are wide-ranging, spreading across the whole spectrum of land-based astronautics — from air defense, through low-level strategic strike and satellite reconnaissance, to the quick-fire response of the Rapid Deployment Force (see unusually camouflaged KC-135 of RDJTF, left). But there is a growing feeling among defense experts that this huge fighting arm, in developing high technology combat aircraft heavily reliant on fixed bases such as that below, is digging its own grave. A Soviet first strike on such bases could cripple the Air Force to such an extent that its retaliatory capability would be nil.

Under another program, the B-52G is being converted to carry AGM-86 ALCM cruise missiles. The first squadron of ALCM-armed B-52Gs became operational at Griffiss AFB, NY, late in 1982, and a total of 104 will receive this armament. From 1986 onwards a total of 96 turbofan-engined B-52H bombers will also be converted into cruise-missile carriers.

Using the current AGM-86B missile, the B-52 force will be able to reach 85 percent of all strategic targets from launch positions outside of Soviet airspace, and beyond the range of many defensive systems. The newer AGM-86C will have greater range, allowing all targets to

be attacked from offshore launch areas and giving USAF planners greater flexibility to deceive the Soviet defences by routing the incoming cruise missiles on deceptive flight paths incorporating major changes of course.

The need to cope with cruise missiles seems to have forced many engineering changes to the new Soviet SA-10 surface-to-air missile system, delaying the latter's entry into service by several years. The development of a Soviet long-range air-to-air missile—perhaps an air-breathing weapon in the class of the now-abandoned Martin Marietta ASALM—seems likely, since the Soviet Union is now thought to

Above: Aerial refueling is a vital part of SAC's operations and confers a global capability on the bomber force. The B-1B (similar to the B-1A seen here) will join SAC in 1985 to replace the B-52s, which are already nearly 25 years old.

be focussing its anti-cruise missile defense efforts on engaging the carrier aircraft before ACLMs have been released.

The B-52G and H models are currently supplemented by 80 B-52Ds. The latter were refurbished between 1975 and 1977, being fitted with improved avionics and radar. During the Vietnam War, the high-explosive payload of these aircraft was increased by modifications to the bomb bay and the provision of external ordnance racks. These aircraft are expected to remain in service until the mid-1980s.

In addition to its nuclear role, SAC also deploys its bombers in conventional roles. B-52s provide maritime-reconnaissance facilities over the Indian Ocean, using Australia for transit facilities. Six B-52s flew nonstop from the USA to Egypt and back in 1981 in support of Exercise Bright Star 82. Each dropped 27 500lb high-explosive bombs during low-level flight over an Egyptian weapons range.

Like most USAF aircraft, the B-52 is equipped for airborne refuelling and supported by a fleet of KC-135 tankers. Up to half of these veterans are being re-engined and fitted with improved refuelling equipment and avionics. These will be supplemented by up to 60 KC-10A wide-bodied cargo-tanker aircraft.

The latter will have a dramatic effect on the ability of the United States to reinforce its allies during a crisis. A fleet of 17 KC-10A could refuel an F-4 squadron flying from the USA to Europe, and carry the associated personnel and ground equipment. To achieve the same result using the KC-135 would involve 40 tankers and a similar number acting simply as transports.

The ability of the B-52 to penetrate the latest Soviet defenses must be limited, despite the

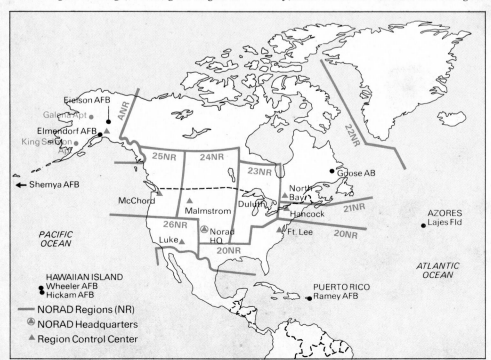

- ▬ NORAD Regions (NR)
- ⊕ NORAD Headquarters
- ▲ Region Control Center

addition of a massive array of internal electronic countermeasures. The CIA has estimated that the aircraft will remain effective until 1990, but more pessimistic studies suggest a date in the mid-1980s. Long-term penetration capability will require the deployment of the "Stealth" bomber currently being developed by Northrop in conjunction with Lockheed and probably becoming operational late in 1990.

In the interim, the USAF intends to deploy 100 B-1B bombers in the mid-1980s. The radar cross-section of this aircraft is only a tenth that of the original B-1 design, and a hundredth that of a B-52, but it seems safe to predict that the aircraft will spend most of its service career as a cruise missile carrier, avoiding the Soviet defences of the 1990s.

A second "stealth" program is known to exist. Prototype hardware has been flown by Lockheed since 1977, and a tactical reconnaissance aircraft similar in size to the F-18 may already be in service. Like the current SR-71 and U-2 aircraft, this may well be operated by SAC.

Faced with the growing threat posed by high-accuracy Soviet ICBMs, the US has upgraded its Minuteman ICBM force to improve survivability. The 450 Minuteman IIIs originally deployed are being supplemented by the modernization of 50 Minuteman II installations to the Minuteman III standard. Missile silos are being modified by the addition of improved suspension for the round, anti-shock mountings for the checkout equipment, additional concrete on the silo lids and the installation of bins on the silo doors to catch debris thrown up by nearby nuclear explosions.

The liquid-propellant Titan II missile is now to be phased out of the SAC inventory. A series of accidents in recent years focussed attention on the weapons' safety and reliability, the force being reduced from 53 rounds to 52 after a silo was destroyed by an accidental explosion.

The failure to establish an acceptable basing mode for the new Peacekeeper missile (formerly

MX) emphasises the problems associated with maintaining a future land-based deterrent. None of the schemes suggested to date combines long-term survivability with acceptable financial or environmental costs.

Command and control facilities for the US strategic forces are partly maintained by a fleet of airborne command posts. The earlier examples are based on the KC-135, but the newer E-4 uses the airframe of the Boeing 747 wide-bodied airliner. When the refurbishment of the first three E-4A Airborne Command Posts to the E-4B standard is completed, these will serve alongside the three examples of the latter standard being built as new aircraft. The B version carries improved command, control and

SAC inventory	
Bombers	
Boeing B-52D Stratofortress	75
Boeing B-52G Stratofortress	151
Boeing B-52H Stratofortress	90
General Dynamics FB-111	63
ICBMs	
Boeing Minuteman II	400
Boeing Minuteman III	600
Martin Marietta Titan II	52
Reconnaissance aircraft	
Boeing RC-135	16
Lockheed SR-71 Blackbird	9
Lockheed U-2R	8
Lockheed TR-1	18
Airborne Command Posts	
Boeing E-4B	6
Boeing EC-135	21
Tankers	
Boeing KC-135 Stratotanker	646
McDonnell Douglas KC-10A Extender	60*

planned

Strategic Air Command units

Headquarters: Offutt AFB, Nebraska

Eighth Air Force (Headquarters: Barksdale AFB, La.)
2nd, 7th, 19th, 68th, 97th, 379th, 410th, and 416th Bomb Wings (B-52/KC-135/KC-10)
380th and 509th Bomb Wings (FB-111/KC-135)
305th and 340th Air Refueling Groups (KC-135)
384th Air Refueling Wing (KC-135)
351st Strategic Missile Wing (Minuteman)
380th and 381st Strategic Missile Wing (Titan II)
11th Strategic Group
306th Strategic Wing
4684th Air Base Group
6th and 20th Missile Warning Squadron
12th Missile Warning Group

Fifteenth Air Force (Headquarters: March AFB, Calif.)
5th, 22nd, 28th, 43rd, 92nd, 93rd, 96th, 319th, and 320th Bomb Wings (B-52/KC-135)
307th Air Refueling Group (KC-135)
100th Air Refueling Wing (KC-135)
44th, 90th, 91st, 321st, and 341st, Strategic Missile Wings (Minuteman)
390th Strategic Missile Wing (Titan II)
6th, 43rd and 376th Strategic Wing
9th Strategic Reconnaissance Wing (SR-71/U-2)
55th Strategic Reconnaissance Wing (RC-135/KC-135)
7th and 13th Missile Warning Squadrons
16th Surveillance Sqn.
46th Aerospace Defense Wing

Below: An ageing B-52D makes a low-level run on an American bombing range. Given the losses over Vietnam, will these old aircraft be capable of penetrating the sophisticated defenses of the Soviet Union?

communications equipment better equipped to survive the effects of electro-magnetic pulse radiation. Airborne refuelling equipment will stretch the maximum mission duration to the 72 hours dictated by the capacity of the engine oil tanks and the endurance of the crew.

Space Command

The USAF set up a Space Defense Operations Center (SPADOC) at the Cheyenne Mountain Complex in Fiscal Year 1980. This was intended to control US space surveillance systems and the two planned anti-satellite (ASAT) squadrons. Formation of USAF Space Command was announced on June 21, 1982 and took place on September 1 of the same year. This is based alongside the existing Aerospace Defense Command facilities at Colorado Springs, Colorado. Several new facilities are planned or under construction.

Main operational unit will be the planned Consolidated Space Operations Center at Peterson AFB, Colorado. This will supervise USAF shuttle missions in the late 1980s and beyond and will back up existing facilities at the Johnson Space Center.

One of the control rooms at Johnson center is

being electromagnetically screened to prevent inadvertent "leakage" of classified data due to stray electromagnetic radiation from computers or other digital data-processing equipment.

Peterson AFB is also the headquarters of 1st Space Wing. Set up in January 1, 1983, this is responsible for the world-wide network of space surveillance and missile early-warning stations originally established by SAC.

Latest of these systems to enter service is the Ground-based Electro-Optical Deep-Space Surveillance System (GEODSS). Tracking stations for this sytem have been built at the White Sands Missile Range, New Mexico, cn the island of Maui in Hawaii, at Diego Garcia in the Indian Ocean and near Taegu in South Korea. Construction of a fifth and final station is due to begin in 1985.

All are equipped with two Contraves Goertz 40 inch (   ) telescopes of 86 inch (   ) focal length. These gather light from the object under

Right: Powerful telescopes probe deep into space from a GEODSS test site at White Sands N.M. America's newest ground-based surveillance system, GEODSS will be fully operational at five sites by 1987.

Major Active Air Force Installations in the US

McChord AFB (MAC)
Fairchild AFB (SAC)
Malmstrom AFB (SAC)
Minot AFB (SAC)
Grand Forks AFB (SAC)
Duluth IAP
K. I. Sawyer AFB (SAC)
Wurtsmith AFB (SAC)
Selfridge ANGB
Kingsley Field (ADC)
Mountain Home AFB (TAC)
Ellsworth AFB (SAC)
O'Hare IAP
Grissom AFB (SAC)
Beale AFB (SAC)
McClellan AFB (AFLC)
Mather AFB (ATC)
Hill AFB (AFLC)
Francis E. Warren AFB (SAC)
Offutt AFB (SAC)
Chanute AFB (ATC)
Wright-Patterson AFB (AFLC)
Travis AFB (MAC)
Lowry AFB (ATC)
Richards-Gebaur AFB (AFCS)
Whiteman AFB (SAC)
Scott AFB (MAC)
Castle AFB (SAC)
United States Air Force Academy
Peterson Field (ADC)
Edwards AFB (AFSC)
Indian Springs AF Auxiliary Fields
McConnell AFB (SAC)
Vance AFB (ATC)
Blytheville AFB (SAC)
Arnold AFS (AFSC)
Vandenberg AFB (SAC)
George AFB (TAC)
Nellis AFB (TAC)
Tinker AFB (AFLC)
Los Angeles AFS (AFSC)
Norton AFB (MAC)
Kirtland AFB (AFSC)
Altus AFB (MAC)
Little Rock AFB (MAC)
Dobbins AFB (AFRES)
March AFB (SAC)
Luke AFB (TAC)
Cannon AFB (TAC)
Sheppard AFB (ATC)
Carswell AFB (SAC)
Columbus AFB (ATC)
Gunter AFS (AU)
Williams AFB (ATC)
Holloman AFB (TAC)
Reese AFB (ATC)
Dyess AFB (SAC)
Barksdale AFB (SAC)
Craig AFB (ATC)
Davis-Monthan AFB (TAC)
Keesler AFB (ATC)
Maxwell AFB (AU)
Goodfellow AFB (USAFSS)
Bergstrom AFB (TAC)
England AFB (TAC)
Lackland AFB (ATC)
Randolph AFB (ATC)
Laughlin AFB (ATC)
Kelly AFB (AFLC)
Brooks AFB (AFSC)
Hurlburt Field (AFSC)
Eglin AFB (AFSC)
Tyndall AFB (ADC)

AB	Air Base
ADC	Aerospace Defense Command
AFB	Air Force Base
AFCS	Air Force Communications Service
AFLC	Air Force Logistics Command
AFRES	Air Force Reserve
AFS	Air Force Station
AFSC	Air Force Systems Command
ALCOM	Alaskan Command

An Air Force Magazine Map

surveillance and feed it to video sensors for conversion into digital data for signal processing and enhancement.

System software is able to differentiate between the light from stars and from man-made objects; the former is automatically filtered out, and the "signature" and position of the spacecraft under surveillance can be checked against a catalog of more than 800 objects which is maintained by NORAD. Some 8,000 to 10,000 observations are made each month, and the results passed to NORAD. In an emergency, data on any suspect object located by the sensors can be passed within minutes to Cheyenne Mountain.

The degree to which GEODSS sensors may examine the physical shape and appearance remains classified, but the fact that such a capability exists was highlighted in 1981 during the first orbital flight of the Space Shuttle. Ground-based cameras were used to examine the lower surface of the orbiting spacecraft to check whether some of the heat-insulating tiles have come loose.

Existing projects involving space weapons and rocket propulsion are now being handled by the Space Technology Center which has been set up at Kirtland AFB, New Mexico.

Tactical Air Command

Tactical Air Command is the arm of USAF which would provide quick-reaction air reinforcements for use overseas. It is currently involved in a major re-equipment program, with the F-15 Eagle and F-16 Fighting Falcon entering service in increasing numbers. Deployment of the A-10 Thunderbolt II ground-attack aircraft has virtually been completed. The ability of the force to survive the Soviet defenses of the mid-1980s and beyond is being enhanced by the massive ECM capabilities of the EF-111A Electric Fox, two squadrons of which are earmarked for deployment in the UK from 1984 onwards.

Most immediate future fighter project is the planned F-4 replacement for the ground-attack role. The service would like to procure both the F-15E version of the Eagle and the delta-winged F-16E, but Congress is likely to insist that a single type be selected.

In the longer term, the USAF wants a Stol Advanced Tactical Fighter capable of operating out of airstrips only 1,000 to 2,000ft (approx. 300 to 600m) long. This demanding specification calls for an aircraft able to cruise at Mach 2 at 50,000ft (15,240m) or Mach 1.6 at low level, have a 700nm (1,290km) tactical radius, and weigh no more than 50,000lb (22,680kg) when

Above: Part of SAC's responsibility is the military side of the Space Shuttle system. From the Orbiter's cargo bay, "spy" satellites will be deployed and retrieved at will.

carrying a 10,000lb (4,536kg) ordnance load.

In the mid-1970s, TAC were able to rely on a large pool of combat-experienced aircrew from the Vietnam War, but had the good sense to ensure that this experience was not lost as these men moved to desk jobs or retired from the service. The massive Red Flag exercises held at Nellis AFB, Nevada, are unique in the West, if not in the world. Flying against typical European targets defended by F-5E "MiG simulators" (Aggressors) and simulated Soviet ground radars, SAMs and anti-aircraft artillery, crews can develop the skills normally won in the crucial first combat sorties which inflict such massive losses on inexperienced aircrew.

Less well known are the Chequered Flag exercises under which TAC squadrons prepare for their wartime deployment to other bases in

Below: A KC-10 Extender refuels a Holloman-based F-15 Eagle. Compared with the more widely used flexible hose system, flying boom tanking is only operational on a large scale with the USAF.

Plattsburgh AFB (SAC)
Loring AFB (SAC)
Griffiss AFB (SAC)
Hancock Field (ADC)
Pease AFB (SAC)
Hanscom AFB (AFSC)
Niagara Falls IAP
Westover AFB (AFRES)
Youngstown Municipal AP
McGuire AFB (MAC)
Greater Pittsburg AP
Rickenbacker AFB (SAC)
Dover AFB (MAC)
Bolling AFB (MAC)
Andrews AFB (MAC)
Washington DC (HQ, USAF)
Langley AFB (TAC)
Seymour Johnson AFB (TAC)
Pope AFB (MAC)
Shaw AFB (TAC)
Myrtle Beach AFB (TAC)
Charleston AFB (MAC)
Robins AFB (AFLC)
Moody AFB (TAC)
MacDill AFB (TAC)
Patrick AFB (AFSC)
Homestead AFB (TAC)

ANGB	Air National Guard Base
ATC	Air Training Command
AU	Air University
IAP	International Airport
MAC	Military Airlift Command
PACAF	Pacific Air Forces
SAC	Strategic Air Command
TAC	Tactical Air Command
USAFSS	US Air Force Security Service

the USA or overseas, Green Flag which focusses on ECM training and tactics, and to other "Flag" exercise programs intended to improve the performance of ground crews and facilities.

With the disbanding of Aerospace Defense Command, TAC is now responsible for the defense of US airspace. SAC still provides long-range warning facilities to guard against missile attack, but TAC mans the small force of air-defense radars, control centers and interceptors which now guards the continental USA. The contrast between this tiny force and the massive defenses which guard Soviet airspace is dramatic: the Soviet Air Force allocates 2,500 interceptors, 1,000 SAM sites with 10,000 missiles and a total of 7,000 radars to air defense; the best that TAC can offer is several hundred interceptors backed up by 120 radar sites. No SAMs are deployed as part of the US air defenses.

Above: Even after 20 years service, the Phantom is still an important type in the TAC inventory. Aerodynamic improvements enable it to continue to match its Soviet rivals. Shrike and Standard ARM hang beneath this F-4G Wild Weasel.

The current USAF interceptor force consists of a single squadron of F-15 Eagles, five F-106 squadrons, plus an F-4 squadron based in Iceland. The Air National Guard provides a further five F-106 squadrons, four units equipped with F-4s, plus one armed with the obsolescent F-101 Voodoo. The F-106s will be

Below: This EF-111 Electric Fox electronic warfare aircraft was originally a standard USAF-operated F-111A. Converted by Grumman along with 41 other F-111s, it now performs the vital task of reducing the enemy's radar capability.

USAF Bases in Europe

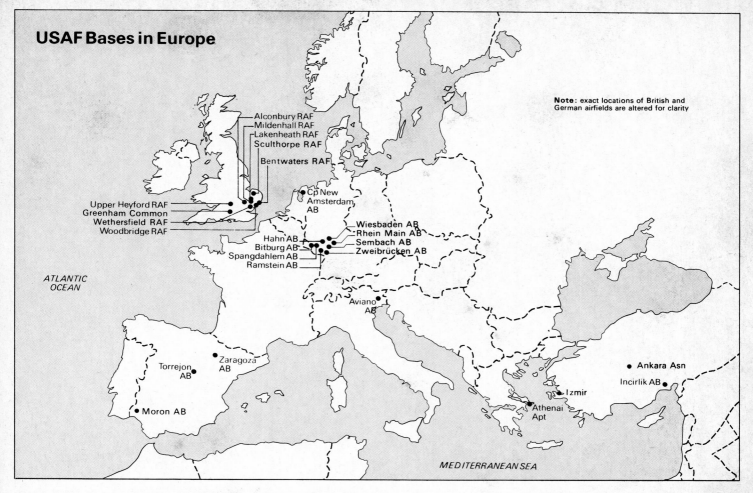

Note: exact locations of British and German airfields are altered for clarity

Alconbury RAF
Mildenhall RAF
Lakenheath RAF
Sculthorpe RAF
Bentwaters RAF
Upper Heyford RAF
Greenham Common
Wethersfield RAF
Woodbridge RAF
Cp New Amsterdam AB
Wiesbaden AB
Rhein Main AB
Hahn AB
Sembach AB
Bitburg AB
Zweibrücken AB
Spangdahlem AB
Ramstein AB
Aviano AB

ATLANTIC OCEAN

Torrejon AB
Zaragoza AB
Ankara Asn
Incirlik AB
Izmir
Moron AB
Athenai Apt

MEDITERRANEAN SEA

phased out and replaced by F-15s, while the F-101 will be replaced by the F-4. The ANG also mans an EB-57 equipped "friendly enemy" unit used to exercise the defenses.

552nd Airborne Warning and Control Wing operates the E-3A Sentry, with squadrons deployed at three bases in the USA and at Keflavik in Iceland, and Kadena in Okinawa. Several E-3s have also been deployed in Saudi Arabia since 1980.

US Air Forces Europe
More than 30 USAF squqdrons serve in the 3rd, 16th and 17th Air Forces which make up the United States Air Forces in Europe (USAFE). Like TAC, these are being re-equipped to meet the threat posed by next-generation Soviet equipment. The F-15C and D replace the earlier F-15A/B standard, while the F-16 is slowly replacing the veteran F-4. First USAFE unit to convert to the F-16 was the 50th Tactical

Fighter Wing at Hahn in West Germany. F-4s made available by this upgrading may now be issued to other USAFE units or US Allies.

The sparsely-equipped A-10 is more suited to US conditions than to the bad weather prevalent in Western Europe, but both this aircraft and the F-16 are due to be equipped with the LANTIRN FLIR system and associated wide-angle holographic HUD.

"Heavy punch" of USAFE remains seven squadrons of F-111E and F-111F strike aircraft based in the UK. Earlier F-111A models of this variable-geometry fighter-bomber have been rebuilt to create the EF-111 Electric Fox ECM aircraft. While the latter jams hostile radars, USAFE's F-4G Wild Weasel aircraft will use APG-38 homing systems to locate and attack radar installations by means of Shrike, Standard ARM or Maverick missiles, plus unguided ordnance such as the Rockeye cluster munition. From 1986 onwards, these will be supplemented

by the new HARM anti-radar missile.

In the long term, USAFE will receive the AIM-120 Advanced Medium-Range Air-to-Air Missile for use against multiple targets at long range, but for the moment will receive interim high-performance weapons such as the AIM-9M version of Sidewinder which offers better acquisition and tracking and improved resistance to countermeasures, plus the AIM-7M "look-down/shoot-down" version of Sparrow. The monopulse radar seeker fitted to the latter is less vulnerable to deceptive jamming than the earlier versions of the missile.

SAC SR-71 Blackbird and RC-135 reconnaissance aircraft are frequent "guests" of USAFE, operating from RAF Mildenhall in the UK. Additional reconnaissance capability is now available in Europe thanks to the deployment in the UK of the TR-1. This will not attempt to overfly hostile territory, but will fly along the border, using sideways-looking radar to gather information. The Precision Location Strike System planned for this aircraft will be able to locate radar systems and direct anti-radar attacks.

Alaskan Air Command
Alaskan Air Command is equipped with the F-15-equipped 43rd Tactical Fighter Squadron and 21st tactical Fighter Wing, plus the close support facilities afforded by the A-10 Thunderbolts of the 18th Tactical Fighter Squadron and O-2 support from the 25th Tactical Air Support Squadron. A total of 13 Aircraft Control and Warning squadrons operate radar sites scattered throughout Alaska's 586,000 square miles (1,500,000km²) of territory.

Pacific Air Forces
New equipment has transformed the front line of Pacific Air Command's 5th Air Force. The Tactical Fighter Wing at Kadena in Okinawa is fully equipped with three squadrons of F-15C/D Eagles plus E-3A Sentries, while the 8th Tactical Fighter Wing at Kusan in South Korea has been equipped with F-16 Fighting Falcons. Osan AB in Korea also operates the new OA-37B FAC aircraft, a rebuilt version of

United States Air Forces in Europe (USAFE) Major Units	
Headquarters: Ramstein AB, W. Germany	406th Tactical Fighter Training Wing (KC-135/range support & weapons training)
3rd Air Force (Headquarters: RAF Mildenhall, UK)	**United Kingdom**
16th Air Force (Headquarters: Torrejon, Spain)	20th and 48th Tactical Fighter Wing (F-111)
17th Air Force (Headquarters: Sembach, W. Germany)	81st Tactical Fighter Wing (A-10)
	10th Tactical Reconnaissance wing (RF-4/F-5)
Main Units	513th Tactical Airlift Wing (C-130/KC-135)
	7020th Air Base Group (KC-135)
Greece	7273rd Air Base Group (GLCM cruise missiles)
7206th and 7276th Air Base Group (support & communications)	7274th Air Base Group (support & communications)
Italy	**W. Germany**
40th Tactical Group (various USAFE aircraft on rotation)	36th Tactical Fighter Wing (F-15)
7275th Air Base Group (support & communications)	50th Tactical Fighter Wing (F-16)
	52nd and 86th Tactical Fighter Wings (F-4)
Netherlands	26th Tactical Reconnaissance Wing (RF-4)
32nd Tactical Fighter Squadron (F-15)	435th Tactical Airlift Wing (C-9/C-130)
	600th Tactical Control Wing (command, control & communications)
Spain	601st Tactical Control Wing (OV-10/CH-53)
401st Tactical Fighter Wing (F-4)	7100th Air Base Group (command, control & communications)
	7350th Air Base Group (support & communications)

the A-37 Dragonfly formerly operated by the US Air Force Reserve.

Military Airlift Command

Even by airline standards, Military Airlift Command is a formidable organization, operating a fleet which includes 77 wide-bodied aircraft, 275 four-engined jet transports and more than 250 four-turboprop freighters. The entire fleet, including the smaller helicopters and transports, numbers almost 1,000 aircraft.

Long-range mainstay of the Command is the C-5 Galaxy fleet. Seventy are being rebuilt with new wings in a program due for completion in 1987, and are expected to serve into the 21st century. USAF would like to acquire 50 new strategic transports, and is likely to receive the C-5B version of the Galaxy. This will incorporate the new wing and improved TF39 turbofans.

In another massive rebuilding program, Lockheed stretched 271 C-141A StarLifters to create the present C-141B fleet. These incorporate a refuelling receptacle located in a fairing mounted on top of the forward fuselage, making the aircraft less dependent on landing rights during wartime resupply missions.

Main tactical transport is the seemingly irreplaceable C-130 Hercules. The mid-1970s YC-14 and YC-15 jet transports were planned as Hercules replacements, but Congress decided that the best C-130 replacement was a new C-130 and the program was allowed to die. Latest projected replacement is the McDonnell C-17 four-jet transport. Although delayed by Congress, this could enter service later this decade.

Aerospace Rescue and Recovery Service (ARRS) at Scott AFB, Illinois, is probably the most exotic MAC unit. Its most publicized activity is combat search and rescue using specially equipped HC-130 Hercules plus Sikorsky HH-3 and HH-53 rescue helicopters. Most complex of the latter is probably the HH-53H Pave Low 3, which carries a comprehensive avionics suite for all-weather rescue missions, including a terrain-following radar, stabilized FLIR plus Doppler and inertial navigation units. These rotary-wing types are due to be joined by the new HH-60D Nighthawk version of the Black Hawk helicopter.

ARRS also flies various models of C-130 and C-135 for weather reconnaissance, air sampling (a means of detecting clandestine nuclear testing), and to support Space Shuttle and Stratetic Air Command operations.

Air Training Command

Approximately a fifth of all USAF sorties are flown by Air Training Command using a fleet of T-37, T-38 Talon, T-41A, T-43A and UV-18B aircraft. The new Fairchild T-46 trainer is due to enter service in 1987 as a replacement for the veteran T-37. A total of 650 are to be built.

ATC handles initial flying training, plus basic military and technical training, but can also handle undergraduate, postgraduate and professional training tasks. Basic flying is handled by 14th, 47th, 64th, 71st, 80th and 82nd Flying Training Wings, while the 323rd Flying Training Wing handles navigator training. All are located in the Central or Southern USA where the favorable climate creates training conditions greatly superior to those found in most European nations. As a result, some non-US NATO air arms send pilots and navigators to the USA for ATC training, such candidates making up about a tenth of the total.

At Sheppard AFB, in Texas, home of the 80th Flying Training Wing, the US and its NATO Allies have set up a Euro-NATO Joint Jet Pilot Training program under which USAF and NATO pilots will train together.

USAF Reserves

The United States is the only nation able to afford large-scale reserve air arms and to equip these with modern aircraft. Like the units of the regular Air Force, Air Force Reserve squadrons have in many cases been upgraded with better

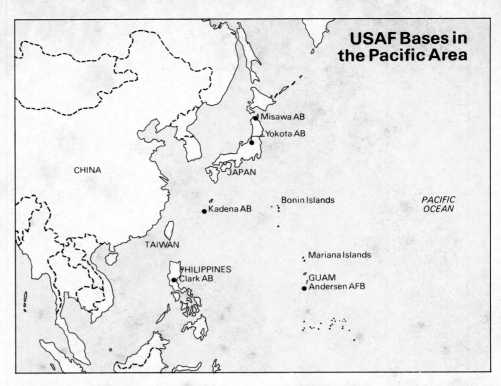

USAF Bases in the Pacific Area

Above: Worldwide political commitments emphasize the need for a large, efficient airlift force and the MAC has almost 1,000 transport aircraft and helicopters. The Hercules forms the tactical element.

Below: Tomorrow's front-line pilots are today's trainees flying such types as the T-38s seen here. A replacement for the T-37 basic trainer has been selected, but what will replace the T-38?

Military Airlift Command fleet (major aircraft)	
Lockheed C-5 Galaxy	77
Lockheed C-141 Starlifter	270
Lockheed C-130 Hercules	259
McDonnell Douglas C-9 (militarized DC-9)	23
Boeing C-137 (militarized 707)	5
Sikorsky CH-3/HH-3	46
Sikorsky CH-53/HH-53	21

USAF strength (Fiscal Year 1983)	
Strategic Bombers	363
ICBMs	1,052
Fighter/attack aircraft	3,026
Reconnaissance & electronic warfare	392
Flight-refueling tankers	544
Transports	828
Helicopters	238
Utility, observation, SAR	250
Trainers	1,664
Personnel (military)	599,000
Personnel (civilian)	243,000

equipment such as the A-10, and are due to receive the F-16. Air Force Reserve is organized into three air forces—4th, 10th and 14th. Main "teeth" flying units are four F-4 squadrons, five A-10 squadrons, two A-7 squadrons, one Wild Weasel unit equipped with the F105D/F, three KC-135 tanker squadrons, and 12 squadrons with the C-130.

The Air National Guard is equipping with ex-TAC F-4s and A-7s and is also receiving some new-production A-7s. The ANG boasts a total of 91 squadrons which make up 17 percent of USAF strength. Main combat types are the F-4C/D, RF-4C, F-105G, F-106, A-7D, A-10, OA-37, C-130 and KC-135.

Inadequacies and Continuing Problems
The contribution of the various US Air Force supporting elements to the combat capabilities of the tactical air forces is significant but difficult to quantify. Easily discernible, however, is the 25 percent Soviet numerical superiority over the US in operational tactical aircraft. Equally visible is the Warsaw Pact's 2-to-1 superiority in ground forces and 5-to-1 superiority over the armored forces of NATO.

To cope with the Soviets' quantitative advantages US tactical air forces are relying on a number of qualitative factors:

Below: Such is the efficiency of the huge C-5A—it can carry almost every type of US military vehicle—the USAF has decided to order a modernized version known as the C-5B with a new wing and engines.

Above: The Hercules replacement? A McDonnell Douglas project, known as the C-17, proposed as a follow-on transport from 1990 for the C-130 and C-141.

Below: Stringent budgetary cuts forced the USAF into "stretching" each of its fleet of 270 C-141 StarLifters. The result was the equivalent of 90 new aircraft.

a continuing, though diminishing lead in technology;

modernization of tactical forces after a long relative lull in production;

superior aircraft such as the F-15 and F-16 which are expected to outperform any opposition throughout the 1980s;

superior capabilities for surveillance, command, control, and communication;

improved defense suppression techniques, especially in the currently marginal electronics countermeasures capability;

balancing costs, quantity and quality through the concept of the high-low mix;

superior capabilities of American precision guided munitions;

more highly trained and combat-experienced personnel;

superior strategic and tactical air mobility to help compensate for potential Soviet geographical advantages;

superior logistics support of combat forces;

superior tactical nuclear capability;

potential reinforcement of tactical forces, under some scenarios, by the conventional or nuclear capability of strategic forces.

Undoubtedly, these factors are impressive to the Soviets. Many analysts believe that they would be sufficient to cope with numerically superior Soviet tactical air forces in the event of war. Less certain is their ability to compensate for Warsaw Pact superiority on the ground. Hopefully, USAF's tactical air forces, under the strategic nuclear umbrella, will not have to prove the point in combat.

Though the American aerospace industry can in general produce better aircraft and supporting hardware than any other country, and certainly can do it quicker, the price is a severe deterrent to any US administration. Even that of President Reagan, which has been trying to rectify the deferred and negative decisions of the 1970s, has had to look for ways to cut $13

Below: The A-10 Thunderbolt might be one of the most heavily armored ground-attack aircraft ever built, but will it survive in a Central Front war in Europe? The pilots say it would; and that it would give a good account of itself.

billion from the defense budget between now and FY84 (Fiscal Year 1984, which ends on June 30 of that year). Several commentators have said that this means actual cuts in "total obligational authority" of roughly twice this amount, and it means that some major programs will have to go.

In the quality of its hardware, and the skill, dedication and professionalism of its people, the USAF has never been as good as today, but in its strength to preserve world peace the picture is rather bleak. Abandonment of the nuclear tripwire policy of the 1955–65 era meant that there had to be immensely powerful forces ready to deter aggression anywhere. As these forces have shrunk, so has the President tried to muster a Rapid Deployment Force intended to make a small but effective sharp cutting edge available within 24 hours almost anywhere. Such a force is ill-adapted to counter either the colossal manpower and firepower of the Soviet Union or the religious fanatics and urban terrorists who have chosen to prey upon American lives and property in recent years. Moreover, for any really large force the USAF would be hard-pressed to provide sufficient airlift. Even if the C-5A did not have to be re-winged, the need for global airlift over intercontinental distances, possibly terminating at austere airstrips, cannot at present be met, and newer types (KC-10s and C-17s) cannot be procured in anything approaching the necessary numbers.

As detailed above, apart from a very small force of some 50 FB-111A bombers, the entire winged strength of Strategic Air Command continues to reside in the remaining ageing B-52G and H bombers, although the need for a modern long-range deterrent aircraft has been self-evident for 20 years, and the only encouragement that can be drawn from the fact that none has been provided is that today the B-70 (RS-70) would not be the optimum aircraft, just as the B-1 will not be the optimum in 1990. So much time has gone by that any B-1 is better than nothing, and the B-1B, if put into the inventory as at present planned from 1986, will restore credibility to the deterrent that has kept the peace for so long.

For the more distant future a "stealth" bomber which has been under study for many

years could be very important indeed, if the US has the will to produce it. The word "stealth" has come to mean an aircraft offering minimal signatures to defensive detection systems. Stealth characteristics can be achieved by a combination of aircraft shape, exterior surface quality, materials and several other factors, most importantly the EW (electronic warfare) subsystems carried on board the aircraft. Surviving in hostile airspace by high flight speed or altitude is no longer viable but, after prolonged effort, stealth technology has

US Territory	456,100
West Germany	36,600
United Kingdom	22,400
Japan & Okinawa	14,200
South Korea	9,300
Philippines	8,500
Spain	4,800
Italy	4,200
Turkey	3,800
Panama	1,800
Canada	250
Saudi Arabia	310
Egypt	80
Other European locations	7,200
Other E. Asian/Pacific locations	300
Other Locations in Western Hemisphere	60
Other locations in Middle East, Africa & Asia	90

Main Overseas Air Bases

Azores: Lajes
Greece: Hellenikon, Iraklion
Greenland: Sondestrom, Thule
Iceland: Keflavik
Italy: Aviano, Cosimo, San Vito
Japan: Kadena, Misawa, Yokota
Netherlands: Camp New Amsterdam
Panama: Howard
Philippines: Clark
S. Korea: Kunsan, Kwang Ju, Osan, Suwon, Taegu
Spain: Torrejon, Zaragoza
Turkey: Ankara, Incirlik, Izmir
United Kingdom: Alconbury, Bentwaters, Chicksands, Fairford, Greenham Common, Lakenheath, Mildenhall, Upper Heyford, Woodbridge
W. Germany: Bitburg, Hahn, Hessish-Oldendorf, Linsey, Ramstein, Rhein-Main, Sembach, Spangdahlem, Tempelhof, Zweibrucken

Above: The best defensive equipment US technology can devise is packed into these SAC B-52s, but massive Soviet defenses could prevent these big aircraft from even getting to their targets.

Below: Phantoms still equip a number of squadrons in USAF Europe, but this large and not-so-young two-seater is now well supported by F-15 fighters and increasing numbers of the smaller F-16.

reached the point at which it dominates the design of offensive aircraft, not excepting cruise missiles. The USAF is now funding at an increasing rate an ATB (Advanced Technology Bomber) which it is hoped will supplement the B-1B in the SAC inventory from about 1992. Northrop's appointment as prime contractor generated slightly misleading speculation that the ATB would be a YB-49 type of flying wing. The California company is teamed with Boeing and Vought, with GE providing the vitally important "zero signature" propulsion.

In the much shorter term Lockheed, which is supplying the TR-1 reconnaissance aircraft designed to non-stealth technology, has for some time been using stealth technology in a relatively small tactical platform called CSIRS (Covert Survivable Inweather Recon/Strike), intended to enter USAF service as early as 1983-4. Using some of the advanced aerodynamics of the SR-71 and GTD-21 RPV, the CSIRS tries to avoid being shot down on multi-sensor reconnaissance and precision attack missions by a combination of high performance and as much stealth technology as could be incorporated in the timescale, for the available budget. It is planned to deploy 20 CSIRS aircraft, with possibly more to follow of a more advanced derived type, but the work is largely classified and cannot be referred to as a regular USAF type in the inventory that follows.

At a totally different level, another machine not included in the following inventory is the Piper Enforcer. Unbelievably, this is derived from the P-51 Mustang, first flown to British order in 1940 and subsequently one of the best fighter/bomber aircraft of World War II and the Korean war. During the Vietnam war it often came into discussion, and Cavalier Aircraft sold almost new-build P-51s to the Air Force and Army, though only in small numbers for training and evaluation. Piper, a leading general aviation builder, was asked to produce a largely redesigned Mustang with a turboprop engine to meet a possible need for a light close-support attack aircraft. Piper announced the start of flight testing of the first Enforcer on 29 April 1971, the chosen engine being the Lycoming T55. Subsequently, Piper made no further announcement, and many observers were surprised when in 1981 the company was awarded a three-year contract, for some $2 million, to fly two further Enforcers with many new features. That there must be a place for a very small, agile, propeller- or fan-engined tactical aircraft, pulling 7g turns at about 300 knots and able to kill tanks and other battlefield targets, appears indisputable. The wisdom of basing it on even a redesigned Mustang is highly questionable.

Today's "Mustang", of course, is the F-16, and this is perhaps the brightest star in the entire Air Force inventory. Out of a very

Above: No base commander would wish to be confronted by this scene in wartime, yet the US fixed basing policy remains one dangerous shortcoming in American defense planning.

limited Light Weight Fighter program, whose main objective was to see if a useful fighter could be made smaller and cheaper than the F-15, has come a tactical aircraft whose limitations are already hard to probe and are being pushed wider all the time. Perhaps the single event that did most to convert the doubters—whose opinion of the F-16 rested on supposed

Below: One of the very few all-weather, low-level strike aircraft available in the West is the F-111. In wartime F-111s are tasked with deep penetration missions into Warsaw Pact territory aimed at hitting airfields and back-area targets.

inadequate avionics, so that it could not do a real job in the bad weather of northern Europe —was the RAF's annual tac-bombing contest held in mid-1981. A team of seven F-16s from the 388th TFW not only won the contest, beating such specialized attack systems as the Jaguar, Buccaneer and F-111F, but set a remarkable new record in scoring 7,831 of the possible 8,000 points. This aircraft will continue to develop for at least the next 20 years, and will probably be the most numerous aircraft in the inventory for most of that time.

Dangerous Basing Policy
Almost the only shortcoming of the F-16, and it is a shortcoming of every other aeroplane in the USAF, is that it is tied to airfields whose precise position is known to potential enemies. Those potential enemies having the capability to do so, such as the Soviet Union, could wipe out those bases in minutes. It is simply a matter of everyday fact that, should it choose to do so, the Soviet Union could suddenly and totally destroy every airfield used by all the air forces of NATO, including every operating base of the USAF. It would then be too late to rectify the folly of not deploying strong forces of V/STOL aircraft dispersed so completely through the countryside—if possible at locations offering natural ski jumps—that no amount of satellite reconnaissance could find them, and the task of destroying them by missiles would be uneconomic.

Since 1960 the USAF's position on V/STOL has been variously negative, non-existent and ridiculous. The fact that the only V/STOL aircraft actually deployed (in the West) has been of British origin has served to warp and diminish USAF interest in the only survivable form of modern airpower.

Billions spent on B-1B, stealth aircraft and even the agile F-16 will be wasted if at 11 tomorrow morning someone presses a button and sends the whole lot up in fireballs as they stand on their airfield ramps. There would then be no longer be any USAF, except perhaps for the planning staffs in the Pentagon and at Air Force Systems Command, who would be left to ponder on where they went wrong. . . .

Above: Small, cheap and available—the lightweight F-16 could be termed the USAF's savior. Over the next 20 years, this combat-proven aircraft will be developed far beyond its present performance envelope. Hill-based F-16s are seen here.

Below: The Eagle is considered to be the match of any Soviet fighter, current or presently projected. However, given Russian numerical superiority of 3–1, these USAFE Bitburg-based aircraft would find the going pretty rough.

Above: One of the USAF's most demanding tasks is long-range strike and deep interdiction, and the F-111 is custom-built for the job; here an F-111A during stores separation tests demonstrates its impressive load-carrying ability with eight pylons fitted

Below: The US Marine Corps has its own special requirements for airpower to support amphibious landings and heli-borne assaults. Starting with the AV-8A Harrier (above), it has developed the AV-8B (foreground) for close support from ship or land bases.

Above: Air superiority is vital in modern warfare, and the F-15 Eagle was designed to keep the skies clear of hostile aircraft. To hone air combat skills, the USAF also operates Aggressor Squadrons, whose F-5Es (foreground) are painted in Warsaw Pact camouflage schemes.

Below: The US Army handed over responsibility for armed fixed-wing aircraft to the newly formed USAF in 1947, but it still operates large — and growing — numbers of helicopters. Most formidable is the AH-64 Apache, designed to tackle and defeat enemy tanks head-on.

US Combat Aircraft

This catalogue includes the major combat aircraft in service with the US armed forces, and important projects under development. They are arranged in alphabetical order of manufacturers' names.

Bell 209 HueyCobra

AH-1G to -1T HueyCobra (data for -1S)

Origin: Bell Helicopter Textron, Fort Worth.
Type: Two-seat combat helicopter.
Engine: 1,800shp Lycoming T53-L-703 turboshaft.
Dimensions: Main-rotor diameter 44ft (13.4m); overall length (rotors turning) 52ft 11½in (16.14m); length of fuselage 44ft 5in (13.54m); height 13ft 5½in (4.1m).
Weights: Empty 6,598lb (2,993kg); maximum 10,000lb (4,536kg).
Performance: Maximum speed (TOW configuration) 141mph (227km/h); max rate of climb (SL, rated power) 1,620ft (494m)/min; service ceiling (rated power) 12,200 ft (3,719m); hovering ceiling in ground effect, same; range (max fuel, SL, 8% reserve) 315 miles (507km).
Armament: M65 system with nose telescope sight and crew helmet sights for cueing and guiding eight TOW missiles on outboard underwing pylons; chin turret (to 100th AH-1S) M28 with 7.62mm Minigun and 40mm M129 grenade launcher with 300 bombs, (from No 101) GE Universal turret with 20mm M197 three-barrel gun (or alternative 30mm); also wide range of cluster/fuel-air explosive and other weapons or five types of rocket fired from 7 or 19-tube launchers.
History: First flight 7 September 1965; combat service June 1967 (TOW-Cobra January 1973, AH-1S March 1977).

Below: *Canned Heat* was a standard early AH-1G, with M28 system and lateral rocket launchers. It served in the Vietnam war with the USA's "Blue Max" 20th Aerial Rocket Artillery.

Development: First flown in 1965 after only six months of development, the HueyCobra is a combat development of the UH-1 Iroquois family. It combines the dynamic parts—engine, transmission and rotor system—of the original Huey with a new streamlined fuselage providing for a gunner in the front and pilot above and behind him and for a wide range of fixed and power-aimed armament systems. The first version was the US Army AH-1G, with 1,100hp T53 engine, of which 1,124 were delivered, including eight to the Spanish Navy for anti-ship strike and 38 as trainers to the US Marine Corps. The AH-1Q is an anti-armor version often called TOWCobra because it carries eight TOW missile pods as well as the appropriate sighting system. The AH-1J SeaCobra of the Marine Corps and Iranian Army has twin engines, the 1,800hp UAC Twin Pac having two T400 power sections driving one shaft. Latest versions are the -1Q, -1R, -1S and -1T, with more power and new equipment. All Cobras can have a great variety of armament.

Above: One of the very latest AH-S TowCobras firing a Tow missile; note flat-plate canopy.

Below: One of the first Tow firings from the first missile-armed version, the interim AH-1Q, probably pictured in mid-1973. Note the revised nose outline caused by the large Hughes TSU (telescopic sight unit) into which the gunner is looking.

Bell "Huey" family

XH-40, UH-1 Iroquois series (Models 204, 205 and 212)

Origin: Bell Helicopter Textron, Fort Worth.
Type: Multi-role utility and transport helicopter.
Engine: Originally, one Lycoming T53 free-turbine turboshaft rated at 600-640shp, later rising in stages to 825, 930, 1,100 and 1,400shp; (212) 1,800 shp P&WC PT6T-3 (T400) coupled turboshafts, flat-rated at 1,250shp and with 900shp immediately available from either following failure of the other.
Dimensions: Diameter of twin-blade main rotor (204, UH-1B, C) 44ft 0in (13.41m), (205, 212) 48ft 0in (14.63m) (tracking tips, 48ft 2¼in, 14.69m); (214) 50ft 0in (15.24m); overall length (rotors turning) (early) 53ft 0in (16.15m) (virtually all modern versions) 57ft 3¼in (17.46m); height overall (modern, typical) 14ft 4¾in (4.39m).
Weights: Empty (XH-40) about 4,000lb (1,814kg), (typical 205) 4,667lb (2,11kg), (typical 212) 5,549lb (2,517kg); maximum loaded (XH-40) 5,800lb (2,631kg), (typical 205) 9,500lb (4,309kg), 212/UH-1N) 10,500lb (4,762kg).
Performance: Maximum speed (all) typically 127mph (204km/h); econ cruise speed, usually same; max range with useful payload, typically 248 miles (400km).
Armament: Seet text.
History: First flight (XH-40) 22 October 1956, (production UH-1) 1958, (205) August 1961, (212) 1969.

Development: Used by more air forces, and built in greater numbers, than any other military aircraft since World War II, the "Huey" family of helicopters grew from a single prototype, the XH-40, for the US Army. Over 20 years the gross weight has been almost multiplied by three, though the size has changed only slightly. Early versions seat eight to ten, carried the occasional machine-gun, and included the TH-1L Seawolf trainer for the US Navy. Prior to 1962 the Army/Navy designation was basically HU-1, which gave rise to the name Huey, though the (rarely used) official name is Iroquois. Since 1962 the basic designation has been UH-1 (utility helicopter type 1). In August 1961 Bell flew the first Model 205 with many changes of which the greatest was a longer fuselage giving room for up to 14 passengers of troops, or six litters (stretchers) and an attendant, or up to 3,880lb (1,759kg) of cargo. All versions have blind-flying instruments, night lighting, FM/VHF/UHF radios, IFF transponder, DF/VOR, powered controls and searchlight. Options include a hook for a slung load, rescue hoist and various fits of simple weapons or armor. Newest and most important of the Model 205 helicopters in US military service is the UH-1H, which remained in production until 1980. Ten have been converted as EH-1H Quick Fix EW (electronic-warfare) machines, but this role has been taken over by the more powerful EH-60A. Two were given augmented avionics and special equipment as UH-1V medevac transports. The US Army plans to retain at least 2,700 improved UH-1Hs beyond the year 2000 for a wide range of duties, and apart from fitting glassfibre composite blades they will be completely upgraded with over 220 new items or improvements including a radar-warning receiver, chaff/flare dispenser, IR jammer, exhaust IR suppressor, radar altimeter, DME and secure communications even in NOE (nap of the Earth) flying. The Model 212 twin-engine helicopter is used by the US Navy, Marines and Air Force (total of 300) with designation UH-1N.

Above: Standard utility model of the Huey in US service (all branches of the armed forces) is the T53-powered UH-1H, two of which are seen on armed assault with M60 guns in the doorway.

Above: Troops of the USA 1st Cavalry (Airmobile) jump from a UH-1D during Operation Oregon in Vietnam in August 1967.

Bell Kiowa and JetRanger

OH-58A to D and TH-57

Origin: Bell Helicopter Textron, Fort Worth.
Type: Light multi-role helicopter.
Engine: (OH-58A, TH-57A) one 317shp Allison T63-700 turboshaft, (OH-58C) 420shp T63-720, (OH-58D) 650shp Allison 250-C30R.
Dimensions: Diameter of two-blade main rotor 35ft 4in (10.77m); length overall (rotors turning) 40ft 11¾in (12.49m); height 9ft 6½in (2.91m).
Weights: Empty (C) 1,585lb (719kg), (D) 2,825lb (1,281kg); maximum (C) 3,200lb (1,451kg), (D) 4,500lb (2,041kg).
Performance: Maximum speed (C) 139mph (224km/h), (D) 147mph (237km/h); service ceiling (C) 19,000ft (5,791m), (D) over 12,000ft (3,658m); range (SL, no weapons, 10% reserve) 299 miles (481km), (D, no reserve) 345 miles (556km).
Armament: Usually none (see text).
History: First flight (OH-4A) 8 December 1962, (206A) 10 January 1966, (production OH-58C) 1978, (D) 1983.

Development: First flown as the OH-4A, loser in the US Army Light Observation Helicopter contest of 1962, the 206 was marketed as the civil JetRanger, this family growing to encompass the more powerful 206B and more capacious 206L LongRanger. In 1968 the US Army re-opened the LOH competition, naming Bell now winner and buying 2,200 OH-58A Kiowas similar to the 206A but with larger main rotor. US Navy trainers are TH-57A SeaRangers, the 36 survivors of this model being supplemented in 1982 by seven more. Since 1976 Bell has been rebuilding 275 OH-58A Kiowas to OH-58C standard with uprated engine, flat-plate canopy to reduce glint, new instrument panel, improved avionics and many minor improvements. Standard armament kit, not always fitted, is the M27 with a

7.62mm Minigun firing ahead. In 1981 Bell was named winner of the AHIP (Army Helicopter Improvement Program) for a 'near-term scout'. The first of five prototype Model 406 AHIP machines should fly before this book appears and a total of 578 existing OH-58As could be rebuilt to AHIP standard with designation OH-58D, at an estimated cost in 1981 dollars of $2 billion. Features include a new rotor with four composite blades driven by a much more powerful T63-type (Model 250) engine, very comprehensive protection systems and a mast-mounted ball with TV and FLIR (forward-looking infra-red), laser ranger/designator, inertial navigation and one or two pairs of MLMS missiles.

Below: Flat glass cockpit panels and IR-suppressed exhaust stacks identify this Kiowa as uprated to OH-58C standard.

Boeing B-52 Stratofortress

B-52D, G and H

Origin: Boeing Airplane Company (from May 1961 The Boeing Company), Seattle, Washington.

Type: Heavy bomber and missile platform.

Engines: (D) eight 12,100lb (5,489kg) thrust P&WA J57-19W or 29W turbojets, (G) eight 13,750lb (6,237kg) thrust P&WA J57-43W or -43WB turbojets, (H) eight 17,000lb (7,711kg) thrust P&WA TF33-1 or -3 turbofans.

Dimensions: Span 185ft 0in (56.39m); length (D, and G/H as built) 157ft 7in (48.0m), (G/H modified) 160ft 11in (49.05m); height (D) 48ft 4½in (14.7m), (G/H) 40ft 8in (12.4m); wing area 4,000sq ft (371.6m²).

Weights: Empty (D) about 175,000lb (79,380kg), (G/H) about 195,000lb (88,450kg); loaded (D) about 470,000lb (213,200kg), (G) 505,000lb (229,000kg), (H) 505,000 at takeoff, inflight refuel to 566,000lb (256,738kg).

Performance: Maximum speed (true airspeed, clean), (D) 575mph (925km/h), (G/H) 595mph (957km/h); penetration speed at low altitude (all) about 405mph (652km/h, Mach 0.53); service ceiling (D) 45,000ft (13.7km), (G) 46,000ft (14.0km), (H) 47,000ft (14.3km); range (max fuel, no external bombs/missiles, optimum hi-alt cruise) (D) 7.370 miles (11,861km), (G) 8,406 miles (13,528km), (H) 10,130 miles (16,303km); takeoff run, (D) 11,100ft (3,383m), (G) 10,000ft (3,050m), (H) 9,500ft (2895m).

Armament: (D) four 0.5in (12.7mm) guns in occupied tail turret, MD-9 system, plus 84 bombs of nominal 500lb (227kg) in bomb bay plus 24 of nominal 750lb (340kg) on wing pylons, total 60,000lb (27,215kg); (G) four 0.5in (12.7mm) guns in remote-control tail turret, ASG-15 system, plus 8 nuclear bombs or up to 20 SRAM, ALCM or mix (eight on internal dispenser plus 12 on wing pylons); (H) single 20mm six-barrel gun in remote-control tail turret, ASG-21 system, plus bombload as G.

History: First flight 15 April 1952; later, see text.

Development: Destined to be the longest-lived aircraft in all aviation history, the B-52 was designed to the very limits of the state of the art in 1948-49 to meet the demands of SAC for a long-range bomber and yet achieve the high performance possible with jet propulsion. The two prototypes had tandem pilot positions and were notable for their great size and fuel capacity, four double engine pods and four twin-wheel landing trucks which could be slewed to crab the aircraft on to the runway in a crosswind landing. The B-52A changed to a side-by-side pilot cockpit in the

Above: While the lower half of the nose is the radome covering the scanner of the main radar, the twin ventral blisters cover the sensor heads of the EVS (electro-optical viewing system), with a steerable low-light TV and a forward-looking infra-red.

Right: In a cost-conscious SAC the expense of deploying the 32ft (9.75m) braking parachute is seldom justfied—though brakes are expensive as well and one thing the B-52 has never had is thrust reversers. This B-52H was pictured in 1981 complete with all the avionic updates including ALQ-153 pulse-doppler blisters on the fin to warn of approaching missiles.

Boeing C-135 family

C-135 Stratolifter and KC-135 Stratotanker family (data KC-135A)

Origin: Boeing Airplane Company (from May 1961 The Boeing Company), Seattle, Washington.

Type: Tankers, transports, EW, Elint, command-post and research aircraft.

Engines: (A and derivatives) four 13,750lb (6,237kg) thrust P&WA J57-59W or -43WB turbojets, (B and derivatives) four 18,000lb (8,165kg) thrust P&WA TF33-3 turbofans, (RE) four 22,000lb (9,979kg) thrust CFM56-1B11 turbofans.

Dimensions: Span (basic) 130ft 10in (39.88m); length (basic) 134ft 6in (40.99m); height (basic) 38ft 4in (11,68m) (tall fin) 41ft 8in (12.69m; wing area 2,433sq ft (226m²).

Weights: Empty (KC-135A basic) 98,466lb (44,664kg), (KC, operating weight) 106,306lb (48,220kg), (C-135B) 102,300lb (46,403kg); loaded (KC, original) 297,000lb (134,719kg), (KC, later max) 316,000lb (143,338kg), (C-135B) 275,000lb (124,740kg) (typical of special variants).

Performance: Maximum speed (all) about 580mph (933km/h); typical high-speed cruise, 532mph (856km/h) at 35,000ft (10.7km); initial climb (J57, typical) 1,290ft (393m)/min, (TF33) 4,900ft (1,494m)/min; service ceiling (KC, full load) 36,000ft (10.9km), (C-135B) 44,000ft (13.4km); mission radius (KC) 3,450 miles (5,552km) to offload 24,000lb (10,886kg) transfer fuel, 1,150 miles (1,950km) to offload 120,000lb (54,432kg); field length (KC, ISA+17°C) 13,700ft (4,176m).

Armament: None.

History: First flight 31 August 1956, variants see text.

Development: Boeing risked more than the company's net worth to build a prototype jetliner, first flown in July 1954. An important factor behind the gamble was the belief the USAF would buy a jet tanker/transport to replace the Boeing KC-97 family, and this belief was justified by the announcement of an initial order for 29 only three weeks after the company prototype flew, and long before it had done any inflight refuelling tests. The KC-135A Stratotanker differed only in minor respects from the original prototype, whereas the civil 707 developed in a parallel programme was a totally fresh design with a wider fuselage, airframe of 2024 alloy designed on fail-safe principles and totally revised systems. The KC-135A was thus a rapid programme and deliveries began on 30 April 1957, building up to a frantic 20 per month and eventually reaching 732 aircraft.

The basic KC-135A has a windowless main fuselage with 80 tip-up troop or ground-crew seats and a cargo floor with tiedown fittings. Fuel is carried in 12 wing tanks and nine in the fuselage, only one of the latter being above the main floor (at the extreme tail). All but 1,000 US gal (3,785 lit) may be

used as transfer fuel, pumped out via a Boeing high-speed extensible boom steered by a boom operator lying prone in the bottom of the rear fuselage. Only one receiver aircraft can be refuelled at a time, keeping station by watching rows of lights along the underside of the forward fuselage. The original short fin was later superseded by a tall fin and powered rudder, and many tankers were given an ARR (air refuelling receiver) boom receptacle. The KC force numbers 615 active aircraft in 35 squadrons, including 80 aircraft in Reserve units. The 100th ARW (Air Refueling Wing) at Beale AFB exclusively uses the KC-135Q with special avionics and JP-7 fuel for the SR-71 aircraft.

NASA tested a modified KC-135 with large winglets, but though these reduced drag by some eight per cent, calculated to save about 23 million gallons (105 million litres) of fuel per year for the USAF tanker force, they have not been fitted to squadron aircraft. Since 1975 lower wing skins have been replaced, extending life by 27,000h per airframe, and in 1983-89 some 300 tankers are being converted to KC-135R standard with CFM56

nose and entered service in August 1954, becoming operational in June 1955. Subsequently 744 aircraft were built in eight major types, all of which have been withdrawn except the B-52D, G and H.

The B-52D fleet numbered 170 (55-068/-117, 56-580/-630 built at Seattle and 55-049/-067, 55-673/-680 and 56-657/-698 built at Wichita) delivered at 20 per month alongside the same rate for KC-135 tankers in support. The B-52G was the most numerous variant, 193 being delivered from early 1959 (57-6468/-6520, 58-158/-258 and 59-2564/-2602, all from Wichita), introducing a wet (integral-tank) wing which increased internal fuel from 35,550 to 46,575 US gal and also featured shaft-driven generators, roll control by spoilers only, powered tail controls, injection water in the leading edge, a short vertical tail, rear gunner moved to the main pressurized crew compartment and an inner wing stressed for a large pylon on each side. The final model, the B-52H, numbered 102 (60-001/-062 and 61-001/-040), and was essentially a G with the new TF33 fan engine and a new tail gun.

During the Vietnam war the B-52D was structurally rebuilt for HDB (high-density bombing) with conventional bombs, never considered in the original design. The wings were given inboard pylons of great length for four tandem triplets of bombs on each side, and as noted in the data 108 bombs could be carried in all with a true weight not the 'book value' given but closer to 89,100lb (40,400kg). Another far-reaching and costly series of structural modifications was needed on all models to permit sustained operations at low level, to keep as far as possible under hostile radars, again not previously considered. The newest models, the G and H were given a stability augmentation system from 1969 to improve comfort and airframe life in turbulent dense air. From 1972 these aircraft were outfitted to carry the SRAM (Short-Range Attack Missile), some 1,300 of which are still with the SAC Bomb Wings. Next came the EVS (Electro-optical Viewing System) which added twin chin bulges. The Phase VI ECM (electronic counter-measures) cost $362.5 million from 1973. Quick Start added cartridge engine starters to the G and H for a quick getaway to escape missile attack. Next came a new threat-warning system, a satellite link and 'smart noise' jammers to thwart enemy radars. From 1980 the venerable D-force was updated by a $126.3 million digital nav/bombing system. Further major changes to the G and H include the OAS (offensive avionics system) which is now in progress costing $1,662 million. The equally big CMI (cruise-missile interface) will eventually fit the G-force for 12 AGM-86B missiles on the pylons; 173 aircraft are being converted and the first 12 became operational at Griffiss AFB in December 1982. Later, probably about 1986, the bomb bays may be rebuilt to carry an ALCM dispenser, and the USAF has an option to have 96 B-52H bombers to carry ALCM from 1984.

Altogether about 340 B-52s remain in SAC's active inventory, 70 being conventional-bomb D-models and 270 the very different and more sophisticated G and H. These equip 17 Bomb Wings all with home bases in the Continental US. A further 187 aircraft are in storage.

Above: The KC-135 tankers represent a vast airlift potential for troops and many items of cargo; this is an RDF exercise.

Left: SAC uses 14 EC-135C airborne command posts, which retain the boom but have TF33 engines and a mass of extra aerials.

engines giving 95 per cent smaller noise footprint, better takeoff and climb and 150 per cent more transfer fuel at long range. Another 18 were re-engined in 1982 with TF33 (JT3D-3B) engines taken from retired American Airlines 707s, becoming KC-135Es.

MATS, now MAC, bought 15 C-135A and 30 C-135B Stratolifter transports, the Bs with fan engines with reversers and much sprightlier performance with less noise and smoke. These remained windowless but had the refuelling boom removed (though retaining the operator's blister) and were equipped for 126 troops or 89,000lb (40,370kg) cargo loaded through a large door forward on the left side. In MATS these aircraft were soon replaced by the C-141. The final new-build versions were the four RC-135A survey/mapping aircraft for MATS and ten RC-135B for strategic reconnaissance. Thus, total C-135 production for the USAF numbered 808, completed in February 1965.

Since then the family has swelled by modification to become perhaps the most diverse in aviation history, the following all being USAF variants: EC-135A, radio link (SAC post-attack command control system); EC-135B, AF Systems Command, ex-RIA (Range Instrumented Aircraft) mainly twice-rebuilt; EC-135C, SAC command posts; EC-135G, ICBM launch and radio link (with boom); EC-135H, airborne command posts; EC-135J, airborne command posts (Pacaf); EC-135K, airborne command posts (TAC); EC-135L, special SAC relay platforms; EC-135N, now C-135N, Apollo range, four with A-LOTS pod tracker; EC-135P, communications/command posts; KC-135A, original designation retained for SAC relay links; RC-135R, special recon/EW rebuilds; NC135A, USAF, NASA and AEC above-ground nuclear-test and other radiation studies; NKC-135A, Systems Command fleet for ECM/ECCM, laser, ionosphere, missile vulnerability, icing, comsat, weightless, boom and other research; RC135B and C, recon aircraft with SLAR cheeks and other sensors; RC-135D, different SLARs and thimble noses; RC-135E, glassfibre forward fuselage and inboard wing pods; RC-135M, numerous electronic installations, fan engines; RC-135S, most M installations plus many others; RC-135T, single special SAC aircraft; RC-135U, special sensors and aerials cover almost entire airframe, including SLAR cheeks, extended tailcone and various chin, dorsal, ventral and fin aerials; RC-135V, rebuild of seven Cs and one U with nose thimble, wire aerials and ventral blades; RC-135W, latest recon model mostly rebuilt from M with SLAR cheeks added; WC-135B, standard MAC weather platforms.

Boeing E-3 Sentry

E-3A

Origin: Boeing Aerospace Company, Kent, Washington.
Type: Airborne Warning and Control System (AWACS) platform.
Engines: Four 21,000lb (952kg) thrust P&WA TF33-100/100A turbofans.
Dimensions: Span 145ft 9in (44,42m); length 152ft 11in (46.61m); height 41ft 4in (12.6m) (over fin); wing area 3,050sq ft (283.4m²).
Weights: Empty, not disclosed but about 162,000lb (73,480kg), loaded 325,000lb (147,400kg).
Performance: Maximum speed 530mph (853km/h); normal operating speed, about 350mph (563km/h); service ceiling, over 29,000ft (8.85km); endurance on station 1,000 miles (1,609km) from base, 6h.
Armament: None.
History: First flight (EC-137D) 5 February 1972, (E-3A) 31 October 1975; service delivery (E-3A) 24 March 1977.

Development: The USAF had been one of the pioneers of overland surveillance platforms, mainly using EC-121 Warning Stars (based on the Super Constellation, and continuing in unpublicized service until almost 1980). During the 1960s radar technology had reached the point at which, with greater power and rapid digital processing, an OTH (over the horizon) capability could be achieved, plus clear vision looking almost straight down to detect and follow high-speed aircraft flying only just above the Earth's surface. One vital ingredient was the pulse-doppler kind of radar, in which the 'doppler shift' in received frequency caused by relative motion between the target and the radar can be used to separate out all reflections except those from genuine moving targets. Very clever signal processing is needed to eliminate returns from such false 'moving targets' as leaves violently disturbed by wind, and the most difficult of all is the motion of the sea surface and blown spray in an ocean gale. For this reason even more clever radars are needed for the overwater mission, and the USAF did not attempt to accomplish it until quite recently.

While Hughes and Westinghouse fought to develop the new ODR

Boeing E-4 AABNCP

E-4B

Origin: Boeing Aerospace Company, Kent, Washington.
Type: Advanced airborne command post.
Engines: Four 52,500lb (23,814kg) thrust General Electric F103-100 turbofans.
Dimensions: Span 195ft 8in (59.64m); leight 231ft 4in (70.5m); height 63ft 5in (19.33m); wing area 5,500sq ft (511m²).
Weights: Empty, not disclosed but about 410,000lb (186 tonnes); loaded 820,000lb (371,945kg).
Performance: Maximum speed, 700,000lb (317,515kg) at 30,000ft (9,144m), 602mph (969km/h); typical cruising speed, 583mph (939km/h) at 35,000ft (10,670m); maximum range with full tanks, 7,100 miles (11,426km); takeoff field length, ISA, 10,400ft (317m); cruise ceiling, 45,000ft (13,715m).
Armament: None.
History: First flight (747 prototype) 9 February 1969, (E-4A) 13 June 1973.

Development: This unique variant of the commercial 747 transport is being procured in small numbers to replace the various EC-135 airborne command posts of the US National Military Command System and SAC. Under the 481B AABNCP (Advanced Airborne National Command Post) programme the Air Force Electronic Systems Division awarded Boeing a contract in February 1973 for the first two unequipped aircraft, designated E-4A and powered by JT9D engines, to which a third aircraft was added in July 1973. E-Systems won the contract to instal interim equipment in these three E-4A aircraft, the first of which was delivered to Andrews AFB in December 1974. The next two were delivered in 1975.

The third E-4A differed in being powered by the GE F103 engine, and this was made standard and subsequently retrofitted to the first two aircraft. In December 1973 a fourth aircraft was contracted for, and this was fitted with more advanced equipment resulting in the designation E-4B. All AABNCP aircraft have been brought up to the same standard and are designated E-4B. The first E-4B (75-0125), the fourth in the E-4 series, was delivered on 21 December 1979. The E-4B has accommodation for a larger battle staff on its 4,620 sq ft (429.2m²) main deck, which is divided into six operating areas: the National Comand Authorities area, conference room, briefing room, battle staff, communications control centre and rest area. The flight deck includes a special navigation station (not in 747s) and crew rest area, essential for air-refuelled missions lasting up to 72 hours. Lobe areas under the main deck house technical controls and stores for on-board maintenance.

One of the world's most costly military aircraft types, the E-4B is designed for unique capabilities. Its extraordinary avionics, mainly communications but including many other types of system, were created by a team including Electrospace Systems, Collins, Rockwell, RCA and Burroughes, co-ordinated by E-Systems and Boeing. Each engine drives two 150kVA alternators, and a large air-conditioning system (separate from that for the main cabin) is provided to cool the avionics compartments. Nuclear thermal shielding is extensive, and among the communications are an LF/VLF using a wire aerial trailed several miles behind the aircraft, and an SHF (super high frequency) system whose aerials are housed in the dorsal blister that was absent from the E-4A. Since November 1975 the sole operational management for the AABNCP force has been vested in SAC, and the main base is Offutt AFB, Nebraska. This is home to the 55th Strategic Recon Wing, user of the EC-135 command posts, but it has not been announced whether the E-4Bs are also assigned to this wing. Planned force is six aircraft, five of which were in use in 1982.

Below: A production E-4A (aircraft 80-1676) seen operating in 1980 on Pratt & Whitney engines before conversion to E-4B standard with F103 engines and the "doghouse" satellite link.

(overland downlook radar), Boeing was awarded a prime contract on 8 July 1970 for the AWACS (Airborne Warning And Control System). Their proposal was based on the commercial 707-320; to give enhanced on-station endurance it was to be powered by eight TF34 engines, but to cut costs this was abandoned and the original engines retained though driving high-power electric generators. The aerial for the main radar, back-to-back with an IFF (identification friend or foe) aerial and communications aerials, is mounted on a pylon above the rear fuselage and streamlined by adding two D-shaped radomes of glassfibre sandwich which turn the girder-like aerial array into a deep circular rotodome of 30ft (9.14m) diameter. This turns very slowly to keep the bearings lubricated; when on-station it rotates at 6rpm (once every ten seconds) and the searchlight-like beam is electronically scanned under computer control to sweep from the ground up to the sky and space, picking out every kind of moving target and processing the resulting signals at the rate of 710,000 complete 'words' per second. The rival radars were flown in two EC-137D aircraft rebuilt from existing 707s, and the winning Westinghouse APY-1 radar was built into the first E-3A in 1975. The first E-3A force was built up in TAC, to support quick-reaction deployment and tactical operation by all TAC units. The 552nd AWAC Wing received its first E-3A at Tinker AFB, Oklahoma, on 24 March 1977, and went on operational duty a year later. Subsequently the 552nd have operated in many parts of the world. It was augmented from 1979 by NORAD (North American Air Defense) personnel whose mission is the surveillance of all North American airspace and the control of NORAD forces over the Continental USA.

From the 22nd aircraft in 1981 an overwater capability has been incorporated, and from No 24 the systems are to an upgraded standard linked into the JTIDS (Joint Tactical Information Distribution System) shared by all US services as well as NATO forces which use 18 similar aircraft. The planned USAF force is 34 aircraft, funded at two per year and due to be complete in 1985.

Left: Costing well over $100,000,000, this E-3A Sentry was delivered to the 963rd AWAC Squadron at Tinker AFB, part of the 552nd AWAC Wing. It has seen service in Saudi Arabia.

Boeing T-43

T-43A

Origin: The Boeing Company, Seattle, Washington.
Type: Navigator trainer.
Engines: Two 14,500lb (6,577kg) thrust P&WA JT8D-9 turbofans.
Dimensions: Span 93ft 0in (28.35m); length 100ft 0in (30.48m); wing area 980 sq ft (91.05m²).
Weights: Empty 64,090lb (29,071kg); loaded 115,500lb (52,391kg).
Performance: Maximum cruising speed 562mph (904km/h); normal cruising speed, about 464mph (747km/h) at 35,000ft (10.67km); range with MIL-C-5011A reserves, 2,995 miles (4,820km).
Armament: None.
History: First flight (737-100) 9 April 1967, (T-43A) 10 April 1973.

Development: Vietnam experience revealed a serious deficiency of facilities for training modern navigators, the only aircraft for this purpose being 77 T-29 piston-engined machines based on the immediate post-war Convair-Liner. In May 1971 the Air Force announced an $87.1 million order for 19 off-the-shelf Boeing 737-200s, with an option (not taken up) for a further ten. The 19 aircraft were delivered in the 12 months from June 1973, and all have since operated with the 323rd Flying Training Wing at Mather AFB, California. Numerous change orders were issued to the basic

Above: Standard navigation trainer, the T-42A has never been named, nor have its engines received a military designation.

737-200, though engines and equipment items are treated as commercial (there is no military designation for the JT8D). There is only a single door and nine windows along each side of the cabin, the floor is strengthened to carry heavy avionics consoles and operating desks, there are additional avionics aerials, and an 800 US-gal (3027 lit) auxiliary fuel tank is installed in the aft cargo compartment. In addition to the two pilots and supernumerary there are stations for 12 pupil navigators, four advanced trainees and three instructors. Training is given under all weather conditions and at all heights, with equipment which is often modified to reflect that in operational types.

Boeing VC-137

VC-137B, C

Origin: The Boeing Company, Seattle, Washington.
Type: Special missions transport.
Engines: Four 18,000lb (8,165kg) thrust P&WA JT3D-3 turbofans.
Dimensions: Span (B) 130ft 10in (39.87m), (C) 145ft 9in (44.42m); length (B) 144ft 6in (44.04m), (C) 152ft 11in (46.61m); wing area (B) 2,433sq ft (226m²), (C) 3,010sq ft (279.64m²).
Weights: Empty (B) about 124,000lb (56,250kg), (C) about 140,500lb (63,730kg); loaded (B) 258,000lb (117,025kg), (C) 322,000lb (146,059kg).
Performance: Maximum speed (B) 623mph (1002km/h), (C) 627mph (1010km/h); maximum cruise (B) 618mph (995km/h) (C) 600mph (966km/h); initial climb (B) 5,050ft (1539m)/min, (C) 3,550ft (1,082m)/min; service ceiling (B) 42,000ft (12.8km), (C) 38,500ft (11.73km); range, maximum payload, (B) 4,235 miles (6,820km), (C), 6,160 miles (9915km).
Armament: None.
History: First flight (civil -120B) 22 June 1960, (-320B) 31 January 1962.

Development: These aircraft bear no direct relationship to the prolific C135 family but were commercial airliners (hence the civil engine designation) bought off-the-shelf but specially furnished for the MAC 89th Military Airlift Group, based at Andrews AFB, Maryland, to fly the President and other senior executive officials. All have rear cabins with regular airline seating but a special midships HQ/conference section and a forward communications centre with special avionics in contact with stations on land, sea, in the air

Above: Most polished aircraft in the world, USAF 72-7000, serves with 89th MAG; when the President boards, it is Air Force One.

and in space. There are special security provisions. The two VC-137Bs were bought as early 707-153s with JT3C-6 engines and were redesignated on fitting turbofan engines. The first VC-137CC (62-6000), a much larger aircraft equivalent to a 707-320B, was the original Presidential Air Force One. It is now back-up to today's Air Force One, 72-7000.

Boeing-Vertol CH-47 Chinook

CH-47A, B, C and D Chinook (data for D)

Origin: Boeing-Vertol Company, Philadelphia.
Type: Medium transport helicopter with normal crew of two/three.
Engines: Two Avco Lycoming T55-L-712 turboshafts rated at 3,750shp (emergency rating 4,500shp).
Dimensions: Diameter of main rotors 60ft (18.29m); length, rotors turning, 99ft (30.2m); length of fuselage 51ft (15.54m); height 18ft 7in (5.67m).
Weights: Empty 23,093lb (10,475kg); loaded (max SL) 53,000lb (24,267kg).
Performance: Maximum speed (33,000lb/14,968kg) 185mph (298km/h); average cruise (50,000lb/22,679kg) 159mph (256km/h); max rate of climb (SL) 1,485ft (455m)/min; range (22,686lb/10,290kg external load) 34.5 miles (55.5km).
Armament: Normally, none.
History: First flight (YCH-47A) 21 September 1961; (CH-47C) 14 October 1967.

Development: Development of the Vertol 114 began in 1956 to meet the need of the US Army for a turbine-engined all-weather cargo helicopter able to operate effectively in the most adverse conditions of altitude and temperature. Retaining the tandem-rotor configuration, the first YCH-47A flew on the power of two 2,200shp Lycoming T55 turboshaft engines and led directly to the production CH-47A. With an unobstructed cabin 7½ft (2.29m) wide, 6½ft (1.98m) high and over 30ft (9.2m) long, the Chinook proved a valuable vehicle, soon standardized as US Army medium helicopter and deployed all over the world. By 1972 more than 550 had served in Vietnam, mainly in the battlefield airlift of troops and weapons but also rescuing civilians (on one occasion 147 refugees and their belongings were carried to safety in one Chinook) and lifting back for salvage or repair 11,500 disabled aircraft valued at more than $3,000 million. The A model gave way to the CH-47B, with 2,850hp engines and numerous improvements, and then to the much more powerful (3,750shp T55s) CH-47C which in 1983 was the standard model, 213 being retrofitted with glassfibre composite blades. In 1976 Boeing Vertol modified three earlier Chinooks to CH-47D standard, and the first production go-ahead followed in 1980. Among 13 major improvements are a new transmission to take the emergency (single-engine) power of the new engines, a new flight deck, new flight-control/hydraulic/electrical systems, a gas-turbine APU (auxiliary power unit), upgraded avionics, single-point pressure fuelling and triple cargo hooks. Normal load limits are 44 equipped troops, 28,000lb (12,700kg) cargo or 24 litters (stretchers) plus two attendants. The USA hopes to rebuild 436 earlier Chinooks to CH-47D standard in 1983-1991.

Below: In theory the CH-47C could bring in several of these M102 light howitzers at a time, because each weighs a mere 3,196lb. (1,450kg). The Army has no alternatives to the gun or the CH-47.

Boeing-Vertol H-46 family

CH-46 and UH-46 Sea Knight

Origin: Boeing-Vertol, Philadelphia.
Type: Transport, search/rescue, minesweeping.
Engines: Two 1,400 or 1,870shp General Electric T58 turboshafts.
Dimensions: Diameter of each three-blade main rotor 50ft 0in (15.24m); fuselage length 44ft 10in (13.66m); height 16ft 8½in (5.09m).
Weights: Empty (KV-107/II-2) 10,732lb (4,868kg), (CH-46E) 11585lb (5,240kg); maximum loaded (KV) 19,000lb (8,618kg), (E) 21,400lb (9,706kg).
Performance: Typical cruise 120mph (193km/h); range with 30min reserve (6,600lb, 3,000kg payload) 109 miles (175km), (2,400lb, 1,088kg payload) 633 miles (1,020km).
History: First flight (107) April 1958, (prototype CH-46A) 27 August 1959, (E) 1977.

Development: The CH-46A Sea Knight was an assault transport carrying up to 25 equipped troops or 4,000lb (1,814kg) cargo. Boeing-Vertol delivered 624 basically similar Marine CH-46 and Navy UH-46 Sea Knights for assault transport, vertical replenishment of ships and utility transport, and (HH-46) sea/air rescue, these entering service in 1964-71. Since 1977 the survivors have been progressively re-equipped with glassfibre composite rotor blades, and the Marines at MCAS Cherry Point are updating their machines to CH-46E standard with the 1,870shp T58-16 engine, 'crashworthy' seats and fuel system and improved rescue system. Boeing-Vertol is expected to deliver 368 kits in 1985-88 to upgrade all surviving machines for reduced-cost service to at least 1999.

Above: An amphibious warfare team marches out to a CH-46D of Marine Corps squadron HMM-164 "Flying Clamors" whose home base is Futenma, Okinawa. All Marine Sea Knights are being totally rebuilt and updated to CH-46E standard by the end of the decade.

British Aerospace AV-8 Harrier I

AV-8A, TAV-8A and AV-8C

Origin: British Aerospace, UK.
Type: Single-seat attack and close-support, (TAV) dual combat-capable trainer.
Engine: One 21,500lb (9,752kg) Rolls-Royce Pegasus 103 vectored-thrust turbofan.
Dimensions: Span 25ft 3in (7.7m); length 45ft 7in (13.89m); height 11ft 4in (3.45m); wing area 201.1sq ft (18.68m²).
Weights: Empty (AV) 12,020lb (5,452kg); maximum (not VTOL) 25,000lb (1,1340kg).
Performance: Maximum speed (SL, clean) over 737mph (1,186km/h); dive Mach limit, 1.3; time from vertical lift-off to 40,000ft (12.2km) 2min 23s; range with one inflight refuelling, over 3,455 miles (5,560km).
Armament: Two 30mm Aden gun each with 130 rounds; external weapon load of up to total of 5,000lb (2,270kg) including bombs, Paveway smart bombs, Mavericks, cluster dispensers, rocket launchers and Sidewinder AAMs.
History: First flight (AV-8A) August 1970, (AV-8C) May 1979.

Development: Adopted in 1969 by the US Marine Corps as a close-support multirole aircraft for use in amphibious assaults, the AV-8A is a slightly Americanized and simplified version of the RAF Harrier GR.3, lacking the latter's inertial navigation and laser nose but with certain US equipment specified by the customer. A total of 102 were supplied, together with eight TAV-8A dual trainers, deliveries beginning in January 1971. Units equipped have always been the training squadron, VMA(T)-203 at MCAS Cherry Point and three combat squadrons, VMA-231, 513 and 542. Attrition has at times been severe, mainly through reasons other than failures of the aircraft, and prolonged and generally very successful operations have been mounted from every kind of ship and shore airfield. In 1979-84 a total of 47 AV-8As have been upgraded to AV-8C standard with life-improving strakes and retractable flap under the fuselage, a liquid-oxygen system, secure voice radio and improved UHF, passive radar receivers facing to front and rear and a flare/chaff dispenser. The C-model is the standard USMC Harrier until the arrival in October 1983 of the Harrier II.

Above: AV-8As in the powered-lift hovering mode prior to being converted to AV-8C standard. It is in this mode that today's AV-8B Harrier II shows to the greatest advantage, the new wing, flaps, inlets and nozzles giving several tons extra lift.

Cessna T-37

Model 318, T-37B, A-37B Dragonfly

Origin: Cessna Aircraft Company, Wichita, Kansas.
Type: T-37, primary trainer; A-37, light attack.
Engines: (T) two 1,025lb (465kg) thrust Teledyne CAE J69-25 turbojets, (A) two 2,850lb (1293kg) thrust General Electric J85-17A turbojets.
Dimensions: Span (T) 33ft 9.3in (10.3m), (A, over tanks) 35ft 10.5in (10.93m); length (T) 29ft 3in (8.92m), (A, excl refuelling probe) 28ft 3.25in (8.62m); wing area 183.9 sq ft (17.09m²).
Weights: Empty (T) 3,870lb (1,755kg), (A) 6,211lb (2,817kg); loaded (T) 6,600lb (2,993kg) (A) 14,000lb (6,350kg).
Performance: Maximum speed (T) 426mph (685km/h), (A) 507mph (816km/h); normal cruising speed (T) 380mph (612km/h), (A, clean) 489mph (787km/h); initial climb (T) 3,020ft (920m)/min, (A) 6,990ft (2130m)/min; service ceiling (T) 35,100ft (10,700m), (A) 41,765ft (12,730m); range (T, 5% reserves, 25,000ft/7,620m cruise) 604 miles (972km), (A, max fuel, four drop tanks) 1,012 miles (1628km), (A, max payload including 4,100lb/1860kg ordnance) 460 miles (740km).
Armament: (T) None, (A) GAU-2B/A 7.62mm Minigun in fuselage, eight underwing pylons (four inners 870lb/394kg each, next 600lb/272kg and outers 500lb/227kg) for large number of weapons, pods, dispensers, clusters, launchers or recon/EW equipment.
History: First flight (T) 12 October 1954, (A) 22 October 1963.
Development: After prolonged study the Air Force decided in 1952 to adopt a jet primary pilot trainer, and after a design competition the Cessna Model 318 was selected. Features included all-metal stressed-skin construction, side-by-side seating in a cockpit with ejection seats and a single broad clamshell canopy, two small engines in the wing roots with nozzles at the trailing edge, fixed tailplane half-way up the fin, manual controls with electric trim, hydraulic slotted flaps and hydraulic tricycle landing gear of exceptional track but short length, placing the parked aircraft low on the ground. The introduction was delayed by numerous trivial modifications and even when service use began in 1957 pupils were first trained on the T-34. Altogether 534 T-37s were built, but all were brought up to the standard of the T-37B, of 1959, which had more powerful J69 engines, improved radio, navaids and revised instrument panel. After 41 had been converted to A-37As further T-37As were bought in 1957 to bring the total of this model to 447. They serve in roughly equal numbers with the advanced T-38A at all the USAF's pilot schools: 12th Flying Training Wing at Randolph; 14th at Columbus (Miss); 47th at Laughlin; 64th at Reese; 71st at Vance; 80th at Sheppard and 82nd at Williams.

The A-37 was derived to meet a need in the early 1960s for a light attack aircraft to fly Co-In (counter-insurgent) missions. Cessna had previously produced two T-37C armed trainers (many of this model were later supplied to Foreign Aid recipients, including South Vietnam in the 1960s and later these aircraft were then rebuilt as AT-37 prototypes (designation YAT-37D) with much more powerful engines and airframes restressed for incrased weights which, in stages, were raised to 14,000lb

(6,350kg). No fewer than eight underwing pylons plus wingtip tanks were added, giving a great weapon-carrying capability whilst offering performance significantly higher than that of the trainer. Redesignated A-37A, a squadron converted from T-37Bs on the production line was evaluated in Vietnam in 1967. Altogether 39 A-37As were built by converting T-37Bs on the line, followed by 511 of the regular USAF production model with full-rated J85 engines, 6g structure, flight-refuelling probe, greater internal tankage and other changes. The A-37 Dragonfly proved valuable in south-east Asia, where many were left in South Vietnamese hands after the US withdrawal. After the end of the US involvement the A-37B was withdrawn from regular USAF service but it continues to equip a Reserve wing and two Air National Guard groups. The AFR's 434th TFW flies the A-37B at Grissom AFB, Bunker Hill, Indiana, and the ANG units are the 174th TFG (Syracuse, NY) and the 175th (Baltimore, Md).

Below: While the A-37B Dragonfly has proved a popular and low-cost light attack platform (camouflaged aircraft) it has never been able to rival its progenitor, the T-37B (unpainted) as a major USAF type. Many are becoming OA-37B FAC platforms.

Fairchild A-10 Thunderbolt II

A-10A, A-10/T, A-10/NAW

Origin: Fairchild Republic Company, Farmingdale, NY.
Type: Close-support attack aircraft.
Engines: Two 9,065lb (4,112kg) thrust General Electric TF34-100 turbofans.
Dimensions: Span 57ft 6in (17.53m); length 53ft 4in (16.26m); height (regular) 14ft 8in (4.47m), (NAW) 15ft 4in (4.67m); wing area 506sq ft (47m²).
Weights: Empty 21,519lb (9761kg); forward airstrip weight (no fuel but four Mk 82 bombs and 750 rounds) 32,730lb (14,846kg); maximum 50,000lb (22,680kg). Operating weight empty, 24,918lb (11,302kg), (NAW) 28,630lb (12,986kg).
Performance: Maximum speed, (max weight, A-10A) 423mph (681km/h), (NAW) 420mph (676km/h); cruising speed at sea level (both) 345mph (555km/h); stabilized speed below 8,000ft (2,440m) in 45° dive at weight 35,125lb (15,932kg), 299mph (481km/h); maximum climb at basic design weight of 31,790lb (14,420kg), 6,000ft (1,828m)/min; service ceiling, not stated; takeoff run to 50ft (15m) at maximum weight, 4,000ft (1,220m); operating radius in CAS mission with 1.8 hour loiter and reserves, 288 miles (463km); radius for single deep strike penetration, 620 miles (1,000km); ferry range with allowances, 2,542 miles (4091km).
Armament: One GAU-8/A Avenger 30mm seven-barrel gun with 1,174 rounds, total external ordnance load of 16,000lb (7,257kg) hung on 11 pylons, three side-by-side on body and four under each wing; several hundred combinations of stores up to individual weight of 5,000lb (2,268kg) with maximum total weight 14,638lb (6,640kg) with full internal fuel.
History: First flight (YA-10A) 10 May 1972; (production A-10A) 21 October 1975, (NAW) 4 May 1979.

Development: After prolonged study of lightweight Co-In and light armed reconnaissance aircraft the Air Force in 1967 initiated the A-X programme for a new-generation CAS (close air support) aircraft. It had never had such an aircraft, this mission being previously flown by fighters, bombers, attack and even FAC platforms, including such diverse types as the F-105 and A-1. Emphasis in A-X was not on speed but on lethality against surface targets (especially armour), survivability against ground fire (not including SAMs), heavy ordnance load and long mission endurance. Low priority was paid to advanced nav/attack avionics, the fit being officially described as 'austere'. After a major competition the Northrop A-9A and Fairchild A-10A were pitted against each other in a flyoff contest throughout 1972, after which the A-10A was announced the Air Force's choice on 18 January 1973. Including six DT&E (development, test and evaluation) aircraft the planned force was to number 733, to be deployed in TAC wings in the USA and Europe, and also to a growing number of AFR and ANG squadrons.

The original A-10A was a basically simple single-seater, larger than most tactical attack aircraft and carefully designed as a compromise between capability, survivability and low cost. As an example of the latter many of the major parts, including flaps, main landing gears and movable tail surfaces, are interchangeable left/right, and systems and engineering features were designed with duplication and redundancy to survive parts being shot away. The unusual engine location minimizes infra-red signature and makes it almost simple to fly with one engine inoperative or even shot off. Weapon pylons were added from tip to tip, but the chief tank-killing ordnance is the gun, the most powerful (in terms of muzzle horsepower) ever mounted in an aircraft, firing milk-bottle-size rounds at rates hydraulically controlled at

Right: Two pairs of AGM-65A Maverick precision missiles are hung on this aircraft of the 354th TFW from Myrtle Beach. It does not have the Pave Penny laser receiver installed on the pylon under the right side of the nose. The 11 pylons are clearly seen.

Below: Funded by Fairchild Republic, this N/AW (night/adverse weather) two-seater never went into production but outwardly resembles the A-10A combat-ready trainer version now forming a small part of the force. N/AW capability is being enhanced.

General Dynamics F-106 Delta Dart

F-106A, B

Origin: General Dynamics Convair Division, San Diego, California.
Type: All-weather interceptor, (B) operational trainer.
Engine: One 24,500lb (11,130kg) thrust Pratt & Whitney J75-17 afterburning turbojet.
Dimensions: Span 38ft 3in (11.67m); length (both) 70ft 8¾in (21.55m); wing area 661.5 sq ft (61.52m²).
Weights: Empty (A) about 24,420lb (11,077kg); loaded (normal) 34,510lb (15,668kg).
Performance: Maximum speed (both) 1,525mph (2,455km/h) or Mach 2.3 at 36,000ft (11km); initial climb, about 29,000ft (8,839m)/min; service ceiling 57,000ft (17,374m); range with drop tanks 1,800 miles (2,897km).
Armament: One 20mm M61A-1 gun, two AIM-4F plus two AIM-4G Falcons, plus one AIR-2A or -2G Genie nuclear rocket.
History: First flight (aerodynamic prototype) 26 December 1956, (B) 9 April 1958; squadron delivery June 1959.

Development: Derived from the earlier F-102 Delta Dagger, the F-106 had a maximum speed approximately twice as high and completely met the requirements of Aerospace Defense Command (Adcom) for a manned interceptor to defend the continental United States. Linked via its complex and bulky MA-1 electronic fire-control system through a digital data link into the nationwide SAGE (semi-automatic ground environment), the 106 served much longer than intended and in fact never did see a successor, despite the continued threat of the manned bomber, though there were numerous engineering improvements and some substantial updates including the addition of the gun (in a neat installation in the missile bay, causing a slight ventral bulge) as well as improved avionics, an infra-red sensor of great sensitivity facing ahead for detecting heat from hostile aircraft and assisting the lock-on of AAMs, and a flight-refuelling boom receptacle. Convair completed many other studies including improved electric power system, solid-state computer, the AIMS (aircraft identification monitoring system) and an enhanced-capability variant for Awacs control. The last of 277 F-106As and 63 tandem-seat F-106B armed trainers were delivered in 1961. Adcom was disbanded in 1980 and the F-106 is now flown only by fighter interceptor units in TAC and in the ANG, assigned to TAC.

Right: F-106As gathered at Tyndall AFB during one of the annual TAC "William Tell" air-to-air combat proficiency meetings. Over 70 per cent of the dwindling interceptor force is now provided by units of the US Air National Guard, based in Massachusetts, New Jersey, Montana, California and Florida.

2,100 or 4,200 shots/min. The gun is mounted 2° nose-down and offset to the left so that the firing barrel is always on the centreline (the nose landing gear being offset to the right).

The basic aircraft has a HUD (head-up display), good communications fit and both Tacan and an inertial system, as well as ECM and radar homing and warning. Deliveries to the 354th TFW at Myrtle Beach, South Carolina, began in 1977, and over 500 have since been received by units in TAC, USAFE (including the 81st TFW in England and 601 TCW at Sembach) and various other commands including the Reserve and ANG. Though relatively slow and ungainly the 'Thud-II' has won over any pilot who might have looked askance at it, and has demonstrated in its first 100,000 hours the ability to do a major job under increasingly hazardous conditions and at the lowest height normally practised by any jet aircraft. Nevertheless attrition at 9 aircraft per 100,000 hours in 1981 was double expectation, resulting in an increase in the overall programme to 825 to sustain the desired force to the mid-1990s. Significantly, half the 60 aircraft in the FY81 budget were two-seaters, which though priced $600,000 higher are expected to effect savings by reducing the demand for chase aircraft.

In 1979 Fairchild flew a company-funded NAW (night/adverse weather) demonstrator with augmented avionics and a rear cockpit for a WSO seated at a higher level and with good forward view. Both the regular and NAW aircraft can carry a Pave Penny laser seeker pod under the nose, vital for laser-guided munitions, and the NAW also has a Ferranti laser ranger, FLIR (forward-looking infra-red), GE low-light TV and many other items including a Westinghouse multimode radar with WSO display. It is probable that during the rest of the decade A-10As will be brought at least close to the NAW standard, while the two-seat NAW might be procured alongside or in place of future buys of the basic A-10A.

General Dynamics F-16 Fighting Falcon

F-16A, B

Origin: General Dynamics Corporation, Fort Worth.

Type: Multi-role fighter (B) operational fighter/trainer.

Engine: One 23,840lb (10,814kg) thrust Pratt & Whitney F100-200 afterburning turbofan.

Dimensions: Span 31ft 0in (9.449m) (32ft 10in/1.01m over missile fins); length (both versions, excl probe) 47ft 7.7in (14.52m); wing area 300.0 sq ft (27.87m²).

Weights: Empty (A) 15,137lb (6,866kg), (B) 15,778lb (7,157kg); loaded (AAMs only) (A) 23,357lb (10,594kg), (B) 22,814lb (10,348kg), (max external load) (both) 35,400lb (16,057kg). (Block 25 on) 37,500lb (17,010kg).

Performance: Maximum speed (both, AAMs only) 1,350mph (2,173km/h, Mach 2.05) at 40,000ft (12.19km); maximum at SL, 915mph (1,472km/h, Mach 1.2); initial climb (AAMs only) 50,000ft (15.24km)/min; service ceiling, over 50,000ft (15.24km); tactical radius (A, six Mk 82, internal fuel, HI-LO-HI) 340 miles (547km); ferry range, 2,415 miles (3,890km).

Armament: One M61A-1 20mm gun with 500/515 rounds, centreline pylon for 300 US gal (1,136 lit) drop tank or 2,200lb (998kg) bomb, inboard wing pylons for 3,500lb (1,587kg) each, middle wing pylons for 2,500lb (1,134kg) each (being uprated under MSIP-1 to 3,500lb), outer wing pylons for 250lb (113.4kg), all ratings being at 9 g.

History: First flight (YF) 20 January 1974, (production F-16A) 7 August 1978; service delivery (A) 17 August 1978.

Development: The Fighting Falcon originated through a belief by the Air Force that there might be a more cost/effective fighter than the outstanding but necessarily expensive F-15. In a Lightweight Fighter (LWF) programme of 1972 it sought bids from many design teams, picked GD's Model 401 and Northrop's simplified P.530 and evaluated two prototypes of each as the YF-16 and YF-17. GD's engineering team created a totally new aircraft with such advanced features as relaxed static stability (a basic distribution of shapes and masses to attain greater combat agility, overcoming a marginal longitudinal stability by the digital flight-control system), large wing/body flare to enhance lift at high angles of attack and house a gun and extra fuel, a straight wing with hinged leading and trailing flaps used to increase manoeuvrability in combat (the trailing surfaces being rapid-action flaperons), fly-by-wire electrically signalled flight controls, a futuristic cockpit with reclining zero/zero seat for best resistance to g, with a sidestick controller instead of a control column and one-piece canopy/windscreen of blown polycarbonate, and a miniature multi-mode pulse-doppler radar. On 13 January 1975 the Air Force announced full development of the F-16 not just as a simple day air-combat fighter but also to meet a greatly expanded requirement calling for comprehensive all-weather navigation and weapon delivery in the air/surface role.

This vitally important programme growth was triggered largely by the recognition that there existed a near-term European market, and in June 1975 orders were announced by four European NATO countries (Belgium, Denmark, Netherlands and Norway). These organized with GD and P&WA a large multinational manufacturing programme which in the longer term has greatly expanded the production base. In July 1975 the Air Force ordered six pre-production F-16As and two F-16Bs with tandem dual controls and internal fuel reduced from 1,072.5 US gal (4,060lit) to 889.8 (3,368). Both introduced a flight-refuelling boom receptacle (into which a probe can be inserted) and provision for a 300 US gal (1,136lit) centreline drop tank and two 370gal (1,400lit) wing tanks. All eight aircraft were delivered by June 1978, by which time the Air Force had announced a programme for 1,184 F-16As and 204 F-16Bs, with the name Fighting Falcon.

Few aircraft have been as excitedly received as the F-16, which by sheer engineering excellence and painstaking development is as close to the optimum combat aircraft as it is possible to get in its timescale. Even so, it was naturally prey to occasional troubles, notably the prolonged stall-stagnation engine difficulty that had earlier hit the F-15 with an almost identical engine. Following intensive test programmes at Edwards, Nellis and by an MOT&E (multi-national operational test and evaluation) team the 388th TFW at Hill AFB, Utah, began to convert on 6 January 1979 and has subsequently not only achieved a string of 'firsts' with the F-16 but has set impressive records in the process. Next came the 56th TFW at MacDill, Florida, followed by the 474th at Nellis, Nevada, the 8th TFW at Kunsan, S Korea, the 50th TFW at Hahn, W. Germany (in USAFE) and the 363rd at Shaw, S. Carolina. Thanks to the large production base and wide international deployment (extending to Israel, S Korea, Egypt, Pakistan and other countries beyond those previously listed) global deployment of Air Force F-16 units is proving exceptionally simple, the aircraft having swiftly attained an exceptional level of reliabity which is enhanced by outstanding maintenance and self-test features.

Enthusiasm by pilots and ground crew has been exceptional, but an event which dramatically highlighted how far the F-16 had come since 1974 was its first participation in a numerically scored inter-service competition. In the searching USAF/RAF contest held at RAF Lossiemouth on 16-19 June 1981 teams of F-16s (388th TFW), F-111s, Jaguars and Buccaneers were required under realistic wartime scenarios to penetrate defended airspace, engage hostile fighters and bomb airfields and road convoys. The F-16s were the only aircraft to hit all assigned surface targets, while in air combat their score was 86 kills against no losses; rival teams suffered 42 losses and collectively scored but a single kill. The F-16 also scored very much better against Rapier SAM threats, while in the ground-crew part of the contest the 388th achieved an average turnround time between sorties of 10½ minutes, including refuelling, loading six Mk 82 bombs and 515 rounds of ammunition. Since its introduction to TAC the F-16 has had the highest Mission Capable Rate in the command, and has been the only multirole aircraft to achieve the command goal of 70%.

In 1982 production had passed 600 aircraft, with plenty of spare capacity at Fort Worth for up to 45 per month if necessary. Though this excellent output was attained by sticking to an agreed standard of build, improvements have been continual, and many more are in prospect. During production the inlet was strengthened to carry EO/FLIR and laser pods, a graphite/epoxy tailplane of larger size was introduced to match increased gross weight (see data), and the central computer and avionics were changed for a much 'expanded package'. Later the 30mm GE pod gun, Maverick missile, Lantirn and AMRAAM advanced missile will be introduced, the new AAM being linked with the programmable APG-66 radar for stand-off interception capability. Later still the striking bat-like SCAMP (supersonic-cruise aircraft modification program) may result in still higher performance with double bombloads.

Opposite top: One of the first block F-16A Fighting Falcons was used in 1981 for the initial evaluation trials of the Hughes Amraam (Advanced medium-range AAM) which was later chosen over a rival from Raytheon. Later F-16s will fire Amraam, which was well into firing trials with fully guided rounds late in 1982.

Right: First of two F-16XL development prototypes (FSD F-16A No 75-0749) in the startlingly successful Scamp programme, which will double range or bombload while reducing field length and improving agility. It could lead to a production F-16E with new airframe and the General Electric F110 (F101DFE) engine.

Below: Two of the 1980 production Fighting Falcons serving with the 8th TFW (Wolf Pack) at Kunsan AB, South Korea. These early aircraft have the original (small size) horizontal tailplanes.

Below: The F-16B dual-pilot trainer has full weapons capability but about 17 per cent less internal fuel. The cockpits are stepped just enough for good instructor view without a periscope, though the half-inch polycarbonate canopy has a metal frame at roughly mid-length, and a metal rear section. The USAF brought 204 in the initial 1,388 F-16s and expects to add another 100.

Below: Visually less striking than the F-16XL above, the AFTI (Advanced Fighter Technology Integration) testbed is at least as significant. A new flight-control system, with ventral canards, enables manoeuvres to be made in any direction without the prior need to point the aircraft in that direction—potentially a great boon for the fighter pilot.

General Dynamics F-111

F-111A, D, E and F, FB-111A and EF-111A

Origin: (except EF) General Dynamics Corporation, Fort Worth.
(EF) Grumman Aerospace Corporation, Bethpage, NY.
Type: A,D,E,F, all-weather attack; FB, strategic attack; EF, tactical ECM jammer.
Powerplant: Two Pratt & Whitney TF30 afterburning turbofans, as follow, (A, C, EF) 18,500lb (8,390kg) TF30-3, (D,E) 19,600lb (8,891kg) TF30-9, (FB) 20,350lb (9,231kg) TF30-7, (F) 25,100lb (11,385kg) TF30-100.
Dimensions: Span (fully spread) (A,D,E,F,EF) 63ft 0in (19.2m), (FB) 70ft 0in (21.34m), (fully swept) (A,D,E,F,EF) 31ft 11½in (9.74m), (FB) 33ft 11in (10.34m); length (except EF) 73ft 6in (22.4m), (EF) 77ft 1.6in (23.51m); wing area (A,D,E,F,EF, gross, 16°) 525 sq ft (48.77m²)
Weights: Empty (A) 46,172lb (20,943kg), (D) 49,090lb (22,267kg), (E) about 47,000lb (21,319kg), (EF) 55,275lb (25,072kg), (F) 47,481lb (21,537kg), (FB) close to 50,000lb (22,680kg); loaded (A) 91,500lb (41,500kg), (D,E) 92,500lb (41,954kg), (F) 100,000lb (45,360kg), (FB) 114,300lb (51,846kg), (EF) 89,000lb (40,370kg).
Performance: Maximum speed at 36,000ft (11km), clean and with max afterburner, (A,D,E) Mach 2.2, 1,450mph (2,335km/h), (FB) Mach 2, 1,320mph (2,124km/h), (F) Mach 2.5, 1,653mph (2,660km/h), (EF) Mach 1.75, 1,160mph (1,865km/h); cruising speed, penetration, 571mph (919km/h); initial climb (EF) 3,592ft (1,095m)/min; service ceiling at combat weight, max afterburner, (A) 51,000ft (15,500m), (F) 60,000ft (18,290m), (EF) 54,700ft (16,670m); range with max internal fuel (A,D) 3,165 miles (5,093km), (F) 2,925 miles (4,707km), (EF) 2,484 miles (3,998km); takeoff run (A) 4,000ft (1,219m), (F) under 3,000ft (914m), (FB) 4,700ft (1,433m), (EF) 3,250ft (991m).
Armament: Internal weapon bay for two B43 bombs or (D,F) one B43 and one M61 gun; three pylons under each wing (four inboard swivelling with wing, outers being fixed and usable only at 16°, otherwise being jettisoned) for max external load 31,500lb (14,288kg); (FB only) provision for up to six SRAM, two internal; (EF) no armament.
History: First flight 21 December 1964, service delivery (A) June 1967, (EF) July 1981.

Development: In 1960 the Department of Defense masterminded the TFX (tactical fighter experimental) as a gigantic programme to meet all the fighter and attack needs of the Air Force, Navy and Marine Corps, despite the disparate requirements of these services, and expected the resultant aircraft to be bought throughout the non-Communist world. In fact, so severe were the demands for weapon load and, in particular, mission range that on the low power available the aircraft had inadequate air-combat capability and in fact it was destined never to serve in this role, though it is still loosely described as a 'tactical fighter'. After prolonged technical problems involving escalation in weight, severe aerodynamic drag, engine/inlet mismatch and, extending into the early 1970s, structural failures, the F-111 eventually matured as the world's best long-range interdiction attack aircraft which in the hands of dedicated and courageous Air Force crews pioneered the new art of 'skiing'––riding the ski-toe locus of a TFR (terrain-following radar) over hills, mountains and steep-sided valleys in blind conditions, in blizzards or by night, holding a steady 200ft (91m) distance from the ground

at high-subsonic speed, finally to plant a bomb automatically within a few metres of a previously computed target.

Basic features of the F-111 include a variable-sweep 'swing wing' (the first in production in the world) with limits of 16° and 72.5°, with exceptional high-lift devices, side-by-side seating for the pilot and right-seat navigator (usually also a pilot) or (EF) electronic-warfare officer, large main gears with low-pressure tyres for no-flare landings on soft strips (these prevent the carriage of ordnance on fuselage pylons), a small internal weapon bay, very great internal fuel capacity (typically 5,022 US gal, 19,010 litres), and emergency escape by jettisoning the entire crew compartment, which has its own parachutes and can serve as a survival shelter or boat.

General Dynamics cleared the original aircraft for service in 2½ years, and built 141 of this F-111A version, which equips 366TFW at Mountain Home AFB, Idaho (others have been reserved for conversion into the EF-111A). It is planned to update the A by fitting a digital computer to the original analog-type AJQ-20A nav/bomb system, together with the Air Force standard INS and a new control/display set. The F-111E was similar but had larger inlet ducts and engines of slightly greater power; 94 were delivered and survivors equip the 20th TFW at Upper Heyford, England. These are to receive the same updates as the A. Next came the F-111D, which at great cost was fitted with an almost completely different avionic system of a basically digital nature including the APQ-30 attack radar, APN-189 doppler and HUDs for both crew-members. This aircraft had great potential but caused severe

Above: KC-135 boom operator's view of an FB-111A of SAC as it comes in for refuelling. It is carrying four SRAM missiles.

technical and manpower problems in service and never fully realized its capabilities, though it remains a major advance on the A and E. The 96 built have always equipped the 27th TFW at Cannon AFB, New Mexico. The F-111F is by far the best of all tactical F-111 versions, almost entirely because Pratt & Whitney at last produced a really powerful TF30 which incorporated many other advanced features giving enhanced life with fewer problems. With much greater performance than any other model the F could if necessary double in an air-combat role though it has no weapons for this role except the gun and if necessary AIM-9. The 106 of this model served at Mountain Home until transfer to the 48th TFW in England, at Lakenheath. The most important of all F-111 post-delivery modifications has been the conversion of the F force to use the Pave Tack pod, normally stowed in the weapon bay but rotated out on a cradle for use. This complex package provides a day/night all-weather capability to acquire, track, designate and

Grumman A-6 Intruder and Prowler

Grumman A-6A, B, C, E, EA-6A and B and KA-6D

Origin: Grumman Aerospace.
Type: (A-6A, B, C, E) two-seat carrier-based all-weather attack; (EA-6A) two-seat ECM/attack; (EA-6B) four-seat ECM; (KA-6D) two-seat air-refuelling tanker.
Engines: (Except EA-6B) two 9,300lb (4,218kg) thrust Pratt & Whitney J52-8B two-shaft turbojets; (EA-6B) two 11,200lb (5,080kg) J52-408.
Dimensions: Span 53ft (16.15m); length (except EA-6B) 54ft 7in (16.64m); (EA-6B) 59ft 10in (18.24m); height (A-6A, A-6C, KA-6D) 15ft 7in (4.75m); (A-6E, EA-6A and B) 16ft 3in (4.95m).
Weights: Empty (A-6A) 25,684lb (11,650kg); (EA-6A) 27,769lb (12,596kg); (EA-6B) 34,581lb (15,686kg); (A-6E) 25,630lb (11,625kg); maximum loaded (A-6A and E) 60,626lb (27,500kg); (EA-6A) 56,500lb (25,628kg); (EA-6B) 65,000lb (29,484kg).
Performance: Maximum speed (clean A-6A) 685mph (1,102km/h) at sea level or 625 mph (1,006km/h, Mach 0.94) at height; (EA-6A) over 630mph; (EA-6B) 651mph (1,042km/h) at sea level; (A-6E) 648mph (1,037km/h) at sea level; initial climb (A-6E, clean) 8,600ft (2,621m)/min; service ceiling (A-6A) 41,660ft (12,700m); (A-6E) 44,600ft (13,595m); (EA-6B) 39,000ft. (11,582m); range with full combat load (A-6E) 1,077 miles (1,733km); ferry range with external fuel (all) about 3,100 miles (4,890km).
Armament: All attack versions, including EA-6A, five stores locations each rated at 3,600lb (1,633kg) with maximum total load of 15,000lb (6,840kg); typical load thirty 500lb (227kg) bombs; (EA-6B) none.
History: First flight (YA2F-1) 19 April 1960; service acceptance of A-6A 1 February 1963; first flight (EA-6A) 1963; (KA-6D) 23 May 1966; (EA-6B) 25 May 1968; (A-6E) 27 February 1970; final delivery 1975.

Development: Selected from 11 competing designs in December 1957, the Intruder was specifically planned for first-pass blind attack on point

surface targets at night or in any weather. Though area ruled, the aircraft (originally designated A2F) was designed to be subsonic and is powered by two straight turbojets which in the original design were arranged with tilting jetpipes to help give lift for STOL (short takeoff and landing). Despite its considerable gross weight—much more than twice the empty weight and heavier than most of the heavy World War II four-engine bombers)—the Intruder has excellent slow-flying qualities with full span slats and flaps. The crew sit side-by-side under a broad sliding canopy giving a marvellous view in all directions, the navigator having control of the extremely comprehensive navigation, radar and attack systems which are integrated into DIANE (Digital Integrated Attack Navigation Equipment). In Vietnam the A-6A worked round the clock making pinpoint attacks on targets which could not be accurately bombed by any other aircraft until the arrival of the F-111. The A-6E introduced a new multi-mode radar and computer and supplanted earlier versions in Navy and Marine Corps squadrons. The EA-6A introduced a valuable group of ECM (electronic countermeasures), while retaining partial attack capability; 27 were built and remain in use. The KA-6D is a conversion of the A-6A for inflight-refuelling tanker missions with a single hosereel and drogue in the rear fuselage; the 62 in service retain attack capability. By far the most costly model, the EA-6B is a complete redesign as the standard Navy and Marine Corps EW (electronic warfare) platform, with a crew of four to manage several major systems of which by far the largest is the ALQ-99 system which groups receiver aerials in the fin pod and high-power jammers in up to five pylon-hung pods each powered by a nose windmill and each tailored to a particular threat waveband. Grumman is expected to build the 102nd and last Prowler in 1986. Current A-6Es, which remain in production with 318 delivered, have the Tram (Target Recognition and attack multisensor) chin turret, and 50 are being equipped to fire Harpoon missiles (six per aircraft).

Right: The small pimple under the nose is the Tram (Target-recognition and attack multisensor) with infra-red and laser equipment, now fitted to most Navy and Marines A-6E Intruders. This one belongs to VA-65 "Tigers", USS *Dwight D. Eisenhower*.

Above: TAC F-111s have always had black undersides, though a new scheme might be introduced; F-111A on Nellis ranges.

hit surface targets using EO, IR or laser guided weapons. The first squadron to convert was the 48th TFW's 494th TFS, in September 1981. Their operations officer, Maj Bob Rudiger, has said: 'Important targets that once required several aircraft can now be disabled with a single Pave Tack aircraft; the radar tells the pod where to look, and the laser allows us to put the weapon precisely on target.'

The long-span FB-111A was bought to replace the B-58 and early models of B-52 in SAC, though the rising price resulted in a cut in procurement from 210 to 76, entering service in October 1969. It has so-called Mk IIB avionics, derived from those of the D but configured for SAC missions using nuclear bombs or SRAMs. With strengthened structure and landing gear the FB has a capability of carrying 41,250lb (18,711kg) of bombs, made up of 50 bombs of 825lb (nominal 750lb size) each. This is not normally used, and the outer pylons associated with this load are not normally installed. The FB

equips SAC's 380th BW at Plattsburgh AFB, NY, and the 509th at Pease, New Hampshire. No go-ahead has been received for numerous extremely capable stretched FB versions.

Last of the F-111 variants, the EF-111A is the USAF's dedicated EW platform, managed by Grumman (partner on the original Navy F-111B version) and produced by rebuilding F-111As. The USA acknowledges the Soviet Union to have a lead in both ground and air EW, and thousands of radars and other defence emitters in Eastern Europe would make penetration by NATO aircraft extremely dangerous. The vast masking power of the EF-111A, which equals that of the Navy EA-6B and in fact uses almost the same ALQ-99E tac-jam system (but with a crew of only two instead of four), is expected to be able to suppress these 'eyes' and enable NATO aircraft to survive. An aerodynamic prototype flew in March 1977, the ALQ-99 was flying in an F-111 in May 1977, and production deliveries began in mid-1981 to the 366th TFW. The Air Force plans to have 42 aircraft rebuilt as EFs, for service with all USAFE penetrating attack units and others in TAC and possibly other commands.

Grumman F-14 Tomcat

F-14A and C

Origin: Grumman Aerospace.
Type: Two-seat carrier-based multi-role fighter.
Engines: (F-14A) two 20,900lb (9,480kg) thrust Pratt & Whitney TF30-412A two-shaft afterburning turbofans; (C) TF30-414A, same rating.
Dimensions: Span (68° sweep) 38ft 2in (11.63m), (20° sweep) 64ft 1½in (19.54m); length 62ft 8in (19.1m); height 16ft (4.88m).
Weights: Empty 39,762lb (18,036kg); loaded (normal) 58,539lb (26,553kg), (max) 74,348lb (33,724kg).
Performance: Maximum speed, 1,564mph (2,517km/h, Mach 2.34) at height, 910mph (1,470km/h, Mach 1.2) at sea level; inital climb at normal gross weight, over 30,000ft (9,144m)/min; service ceiling over 56,000ft (17,070m); range (fighter with external fuel) about 2,000 miles (3,200km).
Armament: One 20mm M61-A1 multi-barrel cannon in fuselage; four AIM-7 Sparrow and four or eight AIM-9 Sidewinder air-to-air missiles, or up to six AIM-54 Phoenix and two AIM-9; maximum external weapon load in surface attack role 14,500lb (6,577kg).
History: First flight 21 December 1970; initial deployment with US Navy carriers October 1972; first flight of F-14B 12 September 1973.

Development: When Congress finally halted development of the compromised F-111B version of the TFX in mid-1968 Grumman was already well advanced with the project design of a replacement. After a competition for the VFX requirement Grumman was awarded a contract for the F-14 in January 1969. The company had to produce a detailed mock-up by May and build 12 development aircraft. Despite sudden loss of the first aircraft on its second flight, due to total hydraulic failure, the programme has been a complete technical success and produced one of the world's outstanding combat aircraft. Basic features include use of a variable-sweep wing, to match the aircraft to the conflicting needs of carrier compatability, dogfighting and attack on surface targets at low level; pilot and naval flight officer (observer) in tandem; an extremely advanced airframe, with tailplane skins of boron-epoxy composite and similar novel construction methods, and one canted vertical tail above each engine; and the extremely powerful

Hughes AWG-9 radar which, used in conjunction with the Phoenix missile (carried by no other combat aircraft), can pick out and destroy a chosen aircraft from a formation over 100 miles (160km/h) away. For close-in fighting the gun is used in conjunction with snap-shoot missiles, with the tremendous advantage that, as a launch platform, the Tomcat is unsurpassed (Grumman claim it to be unrivalled, and to be able—by automatic variation of wing sweep—to out-manoeuvre all previous combat aircraft). Introduction to the US Navy has been smooth and enthusiastic, with VF-1 and -2 serving aboard *Enterprise* in 1974. The export appeal of the F-14 is obvious and Iran is introducing 80 from 1976. But costs have run well beyond prediction. Grumman refusing at one time to continue the programme and claiming its existing contracts would result in a loss of $105 million. For the same reason the re-engined F-14B, with the later-technology and much more powerful F401 engine, was held to a single prototype. In 1975 ongoing production agreements were concluded and by 1983 total deliveries amounted to a useful 468 aircraft, excluding 80 supplied to Iran. The basic aircraft has remained virtually unchanged, though prolonged trouble with the engines has led to the P-414A version of the TF30 which is hoped to improve safety and reliability. This engine comes with the F-14C in late 1983 together with a new radar, programmable signal processor, a new target identification system embodying Northrop's TCS (TV camera set) which has been slowly retrofitted to existing Tomcats since 1981, a laser-gyro inertial system, completely new cockpit displays and completely new threat-warning and internal self-protection jammer system. In 1980-81, as a replacement for the RA-5C and RF-8G, 49 F-14As were fitted with Tarps (tac air recon pod system), containing optical cameras and an infra-red sensor. Because of severe cost-escalation of the 'cheap' F/A-18A the latter is now more expensive than the Tomcat, which is accordingly expected to be expanded from a 497-aircraft programme to a total of 845, delivered at about 24 per year into the 1990s.

Right: This fine picture was taken during the firing trials with 94 of the new Amraam missiles from the Pacific Missile Test Center at Pt Mugu; aircraft 158625 has one Amraam installed.

Below: Formerly the most flamboyantly painted fighters, F-1A Tomcats are being progressively finished in low-contrast grey.

Grumman E-2 Hawkeye

E-2A, B and C Hawkeye, TE-2C and C-2A Greyhound

Origin: Grumman Aerospace.
Type: E-2 series, AEW aircraft; C-2, COD transport.
Engines: Two 4,910ehp Allison T56-425 single-shaft turboprops.
Dimensions: Span 80ft 7in (24.56m); length 57ft 7in (17.55m); (C-2A) 56ft 8in; height (E-2) 18ft 4in (5.59m); (C-2) 16ft 11in (5.16m).
Weights: Empty (E-2C) 37,616lb (17,062kg), (C-2A) 31,154lb (14,131 kg); loaded (E-2C) 51,817lb (23,503kg), (C-2A) 54,354lb (24,654kg).
Performance: Maximum speed (E-2C) 374mph (602km/h); (C-2A) 352mph (567km/h); inital climb (C-2A) 2,330ft (710m)/min; service ceiling (both) about 31,000ft (9,450,m); range (both) about 1,700 miles (2,736km).
Armament: None.
History: First flight (W2F-1) 21 October 1960; (production E-2A) 19 April 1961; (E-2B) 20 February 1969; (E-2C) 20 January 1971; (C-2A) 18 November 1964; growth E-2C, possibly late 1977.

Development: Originally designated W2F-1, the E-2A Hawkeye was the first aircraft designed from scratch as an airborne early-warning surveillance platform (all previous AEW machines being modifications of existing types). Equipped with an APS-96 long-range radar with scanner rotating six times per minute inside a 24ft diameter radome, the E-2A has a flight crew of two and three controllers seated aft in the Airborne Tactical Data

System (ATDS) compartment, which is constantly linked with the Naval Tactical Data System (NTDS) in Fleet HQ or the appropriate land base. The E-2A can handle an entire air situation and direct all friendly air operations in attacking or defensive missions. From the E-2A were derived the E-2B, with microelectric computer, and the C-2A Greyhound COD (carrier on-board delivery) transport, able to make catapult takeoffs and arrested landings with 39 passengers or bulky freight. The final version was the dramatically new E-2C, with APS-120 radar and APA-171 aerial system, with OL-93 radar data processor serving a Combat Information Center (CIC) staff with complete knowledge of all airborne targets even in a land-clutter environment. Though it has an advanced and costly airframe, more than three-quarters of the price of an E-2C is accounted for by electronics. This version entered service with squadron VAW-123 at NAS Norfolk, Virginia, in November 1973. Production was expected to end in 1977, but since then orders have increased the total to 95, delivered at five per year until completion in 1987. In addition two TE-2C trainers are in Navy service. With the original radar aircraft could be detected within a radius of some 300 miles (480km) but the improved APS-125 now fitted can detect cruise missiles at over 115 miles (185km), track more than 250 targets simultaneously, control more than 30 air interceptions (normally by F-14) and give a clear display to the three controllers. An ALR-59 passive detection system detects hostile radio or radar signals at over-the-horizon distances up to more than 500 miles (800km).

Right: One of the key men aboard a carrier is the Landing Signals Officer, here seen on recovery of a Hawkeye from a shore-based training unit practising actual carrier landings.

Above: Seen here taxiing on land with everything folded, the E-2C is one of the most compact aircraft ever built. All E-2Cs in operational US Navy service are embarked in carriers.

Grumman OV-1 Mohawk

OV-1A to -1D, EV-1, JOV, RV

Origin: Grumman Aerospace.
Type: (OV) multi-sensor tactical observation and reconnaissance; (EV) electronic warfare; (JOV) armed reconnaissance; (RV) electronic reconnaissance.
Engines: Two 1,005shp Lycoming T53-7 or -15 free-turbine turboprops; (OV-1D) two 1,160shp T53-701.
Dimensions: Span (-1A, -C) 42ft (12.8m); (-1, -D) 48ft (14.63m); length 41ft (12.5m); (-1D with SLAR, 44ft 11in); height 12ft 8in (3.86m).
Weights: Empty (-1A) 9,937lb (4,507kg); (-1B) 11,067lb (5,020kg); (-1C) 10,400lb (4,717kg); (-1D) 12,054lb (5,467kg); maximum loaded (-1A) 15,031lb (6,818kg); (11B, C) 19,230lb (8,722kg); (-1D) 18,109lb (8,214kg).
Performance: Maximum speed (all) 297-310mph (480-500km/h); initial climb (-1A) 2,950ft (900m)/min; (-1B) 2,250ft (716m)/min; (-1C) 2,670ft (814m)/min; (-1D) 3,618ft (1,103m)/min; service ceiling (all) 28,800-31,000ft (8,534-9,449m); range with external fuel (-1A) 1,410 miles (2,270km); (-1B) 1,230 miles (1,980km); (-1C) 1,330 miles (2,140km): (-1D) 1,011 miles (1,627km).
Armament: Not normally fitted, but can include a wide variety of air-to-ground weapons including grenade launchers, Minigun pods and small guided missiles.
History: First flight (YOV-1A) 14 April 1959; service delivery, February 1961; final delivery (new aircraft) December 1970.

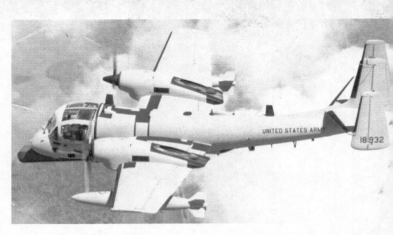

Above: USA OV-1D Mohawks are being reworked and modernized, and also repainted in overall low-contrast grey (see facing page).

Development: Representing a unique class of military aircraft, the OV-1 Mohawk is a specially designed battlefield surveillance machine with characteristics roughly midway between lightplanes and jet fighters. One of its requirements was to operate from rough forward airstrips and it has exceptional STOL (short takeoff and landing) qualities and good low-speed

Hughes AH-64 Apache

Model 77, AH-64

Origin: Hughes Helicopters, Culver City.
Type: Armed helicopter.
Engines: Two 1,536shp General Electric T700-700 free-turbine turboshafts.
Dimensions: Diameter of four-blade main rotor 48ft 0in (14.63m); length overall (rotors turning) 57ft ½in (17.39m); length of fuselage 49ft 1½in (14.97m); height to top of hub 13ft 10in (4.22m).
Weights: Empty 10,268lb (4,657kg); maximum loaded 17,650lb (8,006kg).
Performance: Maximum speed (13,925lb/6,316kg) 192mph (309km/h); maximum cruising speed 182mph (293km/h); max vertical climb 2,880ft (878m)/min; max range on internal fuel 380 miles (611km); ferry range 1,121 miles (1,804km).
Armament: Four wing hardpoints can carry 16 Hellfire missiles or 76 rockets (or mix of these weapons); turret under fuselage (designed to collapse harmlessly upwards in crash landing) houses 30mm Chain Gun with 1,200 rounds of varied types of ammunition.
History: First flight (YAH-64) 30 September 1975; entry into service scheduled 1984.

Development: A generation later than the cancelled Lockheed AH-56A Cheyenne (the world's first dedicated armed escort and attack helicopter), the AH-64 was selected as the US Army's standard future attack helicopter in December 1976. This followed competitive evaluation with the rival Bell YAH-63, which had tricycle landing gear and the pilot seated in front of the co-pilot/gunner. The basic development contract also included the Chain Gun, a lightweight gun (in 30mm calibre in this application) with a rotating lockless bolt. In 1977 development began of the advanced avionics, electro-optics and weapon-control systems, progressively fitted to three more prototypes, followed by a further three—designated Total Systems Aircraft—flown by early 1980. The 56-month development ended in mid-1981, and a production decision was due before the end of that year. Hughes is responsible for the rotors and dynamic components, while Teledyne Ryan produces the bulk of the rest of the airframe (fuselage, wings, engine nacelles, avionic bays, canopy and tail unit). The entire structure is designed to withstand hits with any type of ammunition up to 23mm calibre. The main blades, for example, each have five stainless-steel spars, with structural glassfibre tube linings, a laminated stainless-steel skin and composite rear section, all bonded together. The main sensors are PNVS (pilot's night vision system) and TADS (target acquisition and designation sight) jointly developed by Martin Marietta and Northrop.

Both crew members are equipped with the Honeywell IHADSS (integrated helmet and display sight system) and each can in emergency fly the helicopter and control its weapons. The helicopter's nose sight incorporates day/night FLIR (forward-looking infra-red, laser ranger/designator and laser tracker.

Below: Three of the AH-64 development machines pictured during advanced weapons trials. Speeds up to 237mph (382km/h) have been reached during manoeuvres of these nine-ton battlewagons.

control with full-span slats and triple fans and rudders. Pilot and observer sit in side-by-side Martin Baker J5 seats and all versions have extremely good all-round view and very comprehensive navigation and communications equipment. All versions carry cameras and upward-firing flares for night photography. Most variants carry UAS-4 infra-red surveillance equipment and the -1B carries APS-94 SLAR (side-looking airborne radar) in a long pod under the right side of the fuselage, with automatic film processing giving, within seconds of exposure, a permanent film record of radar image on either side of the flight path. The -1D combined the functions of the two previous versions in being quickly convertible to either IR or SLAR missions. Underwing pylons can carry 150 US gal drop tanks, ECM (electronic countermeasures) pods, flare/chaff dispensers, or, in the JOV-1A such weapons as FFAR pods, 0.50in gun pods or 500lb (227kg) bombs—though a 1965 Department of Defense rule forbids the US Army to arm its fixed-wing aircraft! The EV-1 is the OV-1B converted to electronic surveillance with an ALQ-133 target locator system in centerline and tip pods. The RV-1C and -1D are conversions of the OV-1C and -1D for permanent use in the electronic reconnaissance role. Total production of all versions was 375, and since the mid-1970s the USA has maintained a continuing modernization programme involving (by 1983) 91 earlier models to OV-1D standard, and four to RV-1D, to maintain a force of 110 OV-1Ds and 36 RV-1Ds into the 1990s.

Right: Though this USA OV-1D is painted in the original olive drab it actually looks more like today's medium grey (photo opposite looks falsely white). This particular Mohawk was using SLAR and IR to monitor the Mount St Helens volcanic eruption.

Hughes OH-6 Cayuse and 500M

OH-6 Cayuse, 500M and Defender

Origin: Hughes Helicopters, Culver City.
Type: Light multi-role helicopter.
Engine: One Allison turboshaft, (OH-6A) T63-5A flat-rated at 252.5shp, (500M) 250-C18A flat-rated at 278shp.
Dimensions: Diameter of four-blade main rotor 26ft 4in (8.03m); length overall (rotors turning) 30ft 3¾in (9.24m); height overall 8ft 1½in (2.48m).
Weights: Empty (OH) 1,229lb (557kg), (500M) 1,130lb (512kg); maximum loaded (OH) 2,700lb (1,225kg), (500M) 3,000lb (1,361kg).
Performance: Max cruise at S/L 150mph (241km/h); typical range on normal fuel 380 miles (611km).
Armament: See text.
History: First flight (OH-6A) 27 February 1963, (500M) early 1968.

Development: Original winner of the controversial LOH (Light Observation Helicopter) competition of the US Army in 1961, the OH-6A Cayuse is one of the most compact flying machines in history, relative to its capability. The standard machine carries two crew and four equipped troops, or up to 1,000lb (454kg) of electronics and weapons including the XM-27 gun or XM-75 grenade launcher plus a wide range of other infantry weapons. The US Army bought 1,434, and several hundred other military or para-military examples have been built by Hughes or its licensees. In 1982 Hughes was in production with, or offering, nine military helicopters all significantly

Above: Despite losing to Bell in the AHIP (see Bell Kiowa) the OH-6D as an OH-6A Cayuse rebuild remains an attractive possibility.

uprated compared with the Cayuse, and bristling with advanced avionics, sensors, weapons and protective features, but the only sale to the US military has been USA funding of a single research Notar (NO TAil Rotor) helicopter modified from an OH-6A.

Below: Widely used elsewhere, the Model 500MD with Tow missiles and nose-mounted sight is another OH-6A modification.

Kaman SH-2 Seasprite

UH-2, HH-2 and SH-2 in many versions (data for SH-2D)

Origin: Kaman Aerospace Corp.
Type: Ship-based multi-role helicopter (ASW, anti-missile defence, observation, search/rescue and utility).
Engine(s): Original versions, one 1,050 or 1,250hp General Electric T58 free-turbine turboshaft, all current versions, two 1,350hp T58-8F.
Dimensions: Main rotor diameter 44ft (13.41m); overall length (blades turning) 52ft 7in (16m); fuselage length 40ft 6in (12.3m); height 13ft 7in (4.14m).
Weights: Empty 6,953lb (3,153kg); maximum loaded 13,300lb (6,033kg).
Performance: Maximum speed 168mph (270km/h); maximum rate of climb (not vertical) 2,440ft (744m)/min; service ceiling 22,500ft (6,858m); range 422 miles (679km).
Armament: See text.
History: First flight (XHU2K-1) 2 July 1959; service delivery (HU2K-1, later called UH-2A) 18 December 1962; final delivery (new) 1972, (conversion) 1975, (rebuild) 1982.

Above: An SH-2F Seasprite from HSL-31 (Light helicopter anti-submarine squadron 31) which operates in the training role from NAS North Island (San Diego), California. Note Mk 46 torpedo.

Right: Refuelling at sea in the hover is one of the routines practised by Atlantic Fleet training squadron HSL-32 from Norfolk; this machine is assigned to Knox class frigate *W.S.Sims*.

Development: Originally designated HU2K-1 and named Seasprite, this exceptionally neat helicopter was at first powered by a single turbine engine mounted close under the rotor hub and was able to carry a wide range of loads, including nine passengers, in its unobstructed central cabin, with two crew in the nose. The main units of the tailwheel-type landing gear retracted fully. About 190 were delivered and all were later converted to have two T58 engines in nacelles on each side. Some are HH-2C rescue/utility with armour and various armament including chin Minigun turret and waist-mounted machine guns or cannon; others are unarmed HH-2D. One has been used in missile-firing (Sparrow III and Sidewinder) trials in the missile-defence role. All Seasprites have since 1970 been drastically converted to serve in the LAMPS (light airborne multi-purpose system) for anti-submarine and anti-missile defence. The SH-2D has more than two tons of special equipment including powerful chin radar, sonobuoys, MAD gear, ECM, new navigation and communications systems and Mk 44 and/or Mk 46 torpedoes. All will eventually be brought up to SH-2F standard with improved rotor, higher gross weight and improved sensors and weapons. Though only the interim LAMPS platform the SH-2 is a substantial programme. The first of 88 new SH-2F Seasprites became operational with squadron HSL-33 in mid-1973, and 88 were delivered by the end of the decade. Kaman has since been rebuilding the earlier SH- and HH-2D helicopters to the same configuration, this being completed in March 1982. By this time 220 SH-2D or -2F detachments had served on long ocean cruises aboard eight classes of surface warship, the DD-963 and FFG-7 class vessels having two LAMPS helicopters each. Though LAMPS III (SH-60B) is now entering service the SH-2F will remain operational throughout the 1990s.

Lockheed C-5A Galaxy

C-5A

Origin: Lockheed-Georgia Company, Marietta, Ga.
Type: Heavy strategic airlift transport.
Powerplant: Four 41,000lb (18,597kg) thrust General Electric TF39-1 turbofans.
Dimensions: Span 222ft 8½in (67.88m); length 247ft 10in (75.54m); height 65ft 1½in (19.85m); wing area 6,200sq ft (576.0m²).
Weights: Empty (basic operating) 337,937lb (153,285kg), loaded (2,25g) 769,000lb (348,810kg).
Performance: Maximum speed (max weight, 25,000ft/7,620m) 571mph (760km/h); normal long-range cruising speed, 518mph (834km/h); initial climb at max wt., rated thrust, 1,800ft (549m)/min; service ceiling, (615,000lb/278,950kg) 34,000ft (10.36km); range with design payload of 220, 967lb (100,228kg), 3,749 miles (6,033km); range with 112,600lb (51,074kg) payload 6,529 miles (10,507km); ferry range 7,991 miles (12,860km); takeoff distance at max wt. over 50ft (15m), 8,400ft (2,560m); landing from 50ft (15m), 3,600ft (1,097m).
Armament: None.
History: First flight 30 June 1968; service delivery, 17 December 1969; final delivery from new, May 1973.

Above: Looking like a stranded whale, this C-5A is just opening its nose to disgorge heavy cargo. The leading edges are drooped in this photograph taken at a MAC base.

Right: The C-5A is one of very few aircraft in the USAF which dwarfs the KC-10A Extender, seen here during the latter's first air-refuelling hook-up with a Galaxy. C-5A is aircraft 69-0013.

Development: Growing appreciation of the need for an extremely large logistics transport to permit deployment of the heaviest hardware items on a global basis led in 1963 to the CX-HLS (Heavy Logistics System) specification calling for a payload of 250,000lb (113,400kg) over a coast-to-coast range and half this load over the extremely challenging unrefuelled range of 8,000 miles (12,875km); it also demanded the abililty to fly such loads into a 4,000ft (1,220m) rough forward airstrip. Such performance was theoretically possible using a new species of turbofan, of high bypass ratio, much more powerful than existing engines. In August 1965 GE won the engine contract, and two months later Lockheed won the C-5A aircraft. Design was undertaken under extreme pressure, the wing being assigned to CDI, a group of British engineers from the cancelled HS.115 and TSR.2 programmes. About half the value of each airframe was subcontracted to suppliers in the US and Canada, and construction of the first aircraft (66-8303) began as early as August 1966.

Meeting the requirements proved impossible, and cost-inflation reduced the total buy from 115 (six squadrons) to 81 (four squadrons), of which 30 were delivered by the end of 1970. As a cargo airlifter the C-5A proved in a class of its own, with main-deck width of 19ft (5.79m) and full-section access at front and rear. The upper deck houses the flight crew of five, a rest area for a further 15 and a rear (aft of the wing) area with 75 seats. Features include high-lift slats and flaps, an air-refuelling receptacle, advanced forward-looking radars and a unique landing gear with 28 wheels offering the required 'high flotation' for unpaved surfaces, as well as free castoring to facilitate ground manoeuvring, an offset (20° to left or right) swivelling capability for use in crosswinds, fully modulating anti-skid brakes and the ability to kneel to bring the main deck close to the ground. Despite highly publicized faults, most of which were quickly rectified, the C-5A was soon giving invaluable service; but a deep-rooted difficulty was that the wing accrued fatigue damage much more rapidly than had been predicted. Several costly modification programmes proved incomplete solutions, and in 1978 Lockheed's proposal for the introduction of a new wing was accepted. This wing uses a totally different detailed design in different materials, and though the moving surfaces are largely unchanged even these are to be manufactured again, the slats, ailerons and flap tracks for the second time being assigned to Canadair. Between 1982-87 all 77 surviving aircraft are to be re-winged. This is being done with minimal reduction in airlift capability by MAC's 60th MAW at Travis, 436th at Dover, Delaware, and 443rd at Altus AFB, Oklahoma.

In 1982 the Reagan administration recommended purchase of an additional 50 aircraft costing $8 billion, instead of C-17s. These C-5Ns will have long crack-free airframe life, improved avionics and easier serviceability, but will have performance essentially identical to the existing aircraft. Engines will be TF39-1Cs with modifications purely to increase life and reduce cost. In USAF service the designation of the C-5N will be C-5B, and deliveries are expected at a modest rate from 1988.

Lockheed C-130 Hercules

C-130A to C-130R (sub-variants, see text)

Origin: Lockheed-Georgia Company, Marietta, Ga.
Type: Originally, multirole airlift transport; special variants, see text.
Powerplant: Four Allison T56 turboprops, (B and E families) 4,050ehp T56-7, (H family) 4,910ehp T56-15 flat-rated at 4,508ehp.
Dimensions: Span 132ft 7in (40.41m); length (basic) 97ft 9in (29.79m), (HC-130H, arms spread) 106ft 4in (32.41m); wing area 1,745sq ft (162.12m²).
Weights: Empty (basic E, H) 72,892lb (33,063kg); operating weight (H) 75,832lb (34,397kg); loaded (E,H) 155,000lb (70,310kg), max overload 175,000lb (79,380kg).
Performance: Maximum speed at 175,000lb (E, H), also max cruising speed, 386mph (621km/h); economical cruise, 345mph (556km/h); initial SL climb (E) 1,830ft (558m)/min, (H) 1,900ft (579m)/min; service ceiling at 155,000lb, (E) 23,000ft (7,010m), (H) 26,500ft (8,075m); range (H with max payload of 43,399lb (19,685kg) 2,487 miles (4,002km); 4,606 miles (7,412km); takeoff to 50ft (15m) (H at 175,000lb), 5,160ft (1,573m); landing from 50ft (15m) (H at 100,000lb/45,360kg), 2,700ft (823m).
Armament: Normally none.
History: First flight (YC-130A) 23 August 1954, (production C-130A) 7 April 1955; service delivery December 1956.

Development: When the Berlin Airlift and Korean war highlighted the need for more capable military transport aircraft, several obvious features were waiting to be combined in one design. Among these were a high wing and unobstructed cargo compartment, a flat level floor at truck-bed height above the ground, pressurization and air-conditioning, full-section rear door and vehicle ramp, turboprop propulsion for high performance, a modern flight deck with all-round vision, and retractable landing gear with 'high flotation' tyres for use from unprepared airstrips. All were incorporated in the Lockheed Model 82 which in June 1951 won an Air Force requirement for a new and versatile transport for TAC. By sheer good fortune the Allison single-shaft T56 turboprop matured at precisely the right time, along with a new species of advanced Aeroproducts or HamStan propeller and several other new-technology items including high-strength 2024 aluminium alloy, machined skin planks for the wings and cargo floor, metal/metal bonding and titanium alloys for the nacelles and flap skins. Another new feature was a miniature APU (auxiliary power unit) in one of the landing-gear blisters to provide ground power for air-conditioning and main-engine pneumatic starting.

Two YC-130 prototypes were built at Burbank, with 3,250hp T56-1 engines, but long before these were completed the programme was moved to the vast Government Plant 6 in Georgia which had been built to produce the B-29 under Bell management and restored to active use by Lockheed in January 1951. The new transport was ordered as the C-130A in September 1952 and the work phased in well with the tapering off of the B-47. When the 130, soon dubbed the Herky-bird, joined the 463rd Troop Carrier Wing at Ardmore in 1956 it caused a stir of a kind never before associated with a mere cargo transport. Pilots began to fly their big airlifters like fighters, and to explore the limits of what appeared to be an aircraft so willing it would do impossible demands. This was despite increases in permitted gross weight

Above: Delivery of an M551 Sheridan light Shillelagh-firing tank by the ground-proximity (no parachute) extraction method.

Below: The remaining first-line user of the AC-130H is the 1st Special Ops Wing (TAC 9th AF) at Hurlburt Field, Florida.

Lockheed C-141 StarLifter

C-141A and B

Origin: Lockheed-Georgia Company, Marietta, Ga.
Type: Strategic airlift and aeromedical transport.
Powerplant: Four 21,000lb (9,525kg) thrust Pratt & Whitney TF33-7 turbofans.
Dimensions: Span 159ft 11in (48.74m); length (A) 145ft. 0in (44.2m), (B) 168ft 3½in (51.29m); wing area 3,228sq. ft (299.9m²).
Weights: Empty (A) 133,733lb (60,678kg), (B) 148,120lb (67,186kg); loaded (A) 316,600lb (143,600kg), (B) 343,000lb (155,585kg).
Performance: Maximum speed (A) 571mph (919km/h), (B, also max cruising speed) 566mph (910km/h); long-range cruising speed (both) 495mph (796km/h), initial climb (A) 3,100ft (945m)/min, (B) 2,920ft (890m)/min; service ceiling, 41,600ft (12,68km), range with maximum payload of (A, 70,847lb/32,136kg) 4,080 miles (6,565km), (B, 90,880lb/41,222kg) 2,935 miles (4,725km); takeoff to 50ft (15m) (B) 5,800ft (1,768m).
Armament: None.
History: First flight 17 December 1963; service delivery 19 October 1964; first flight of C-141B, 24 March 1977.

Development: In the late 1950s MATS (now MAC) anticipated a severe future shortage of long-range airlift capacity, the C-133 being an interim propeller aircraft and the much larger C-132 being cancelled. As interim solutions orders were placed for the C-135 jet and for a long-range version of the C-130, but on 4 May 1960 a requirement was issued for a purpose-designed transport which was won by Lockheed's Model 300 submission in March 1961. Ordered at once as the C-141, it followed the lines of the C-130, and even had the same 10ft x 9ft (3.1 x 2.77m) body cross-section (a choice which perhaps proved erroneous, as from the start the internal cube volume was totally inadequate for the available weightlifting ability). The

Above: A pre-modification StarLifter, a C-141A of 438th MAW, McGuire AFB, NJ; compare it with the stretched version, C-141B shown far right.

C-141 was, in other respects, much larger, with a wing of almost twice the area, swept at only 23° (¼-chord) for good field length but resulting in lower speeds than equivalent civil transports. Features included a full-section

from 102,000lb to 116,000 and then to 124,200lb (56,335kg). At an early stage the nose grew a characteristic pimple from switching to the APN-59 radar, and provision was made for eight 1,000lb (454kg) Aerojet assisted takeoff rockets to be clipped to the sides of the fuselage, to augment the thrust of full-rated 3,750hp engines.

In December 1958 Lockheed flew the first extended-range C-130B with more powerful engines driving four-blade propellers. The Air Force bought 132 to supplement the 204 A-models, the latter progressively being rebuilt as AC-130 gunships, DC-130 drone (RPV) controllers, JC-130 spacecraft tracking and retrieval aircraft and C-130D wheel/ski aircraft with Arctic/Antarctic equipment. The next basic model, and bought in largest numbers (389), was the E, first flown on 25 August 1961. With this a minor structural rework enabled wing pylons to carry large drop tanks of 1,360 US gal (5,145lit), meeting the strategic range requirements of MATS (now MAC) and thus opening up a new market for the 130 beyond the tactical sphere. MATS (MAC) received 130 of the E model, and TAC re-equipped with 245 and transferred the A and B models to the ANG and Reserve, giving these reserve forces undreamed-of airlift capability. Some B-models were converted for other roles, new duties including weather reconnaissance (WC-130) and a single STOL aircraft with extra pod-mounted T56 engines supplying a boundary-layer control system, designated NC-130. Among currently serving rebuilds of the E are the EC-130E tactical command and control platform, with several unique avionic systems, and the MC-130E used with special avionics and low-level flight techniques for clandestine exfiltration and airdrop missions.

Latest basic type is the C-130H, first delivered in April 1975, with more

Left: Landing lights aglow, an HC-130H of the USAF Aerospace Rescue and Recovery Service is marshalled during a winter exercise. Some versions have heated ski/wheel landing gears.

Above: The 7th Airborne Command and Control Sqn at Keesler AFB, Mississippi, is an operator of the EC-130E battlefield command/control platform with 20 communications systems.

powerful engines flat-rated at the previous level to give improved takeoff from hot/high airstrips. Variations include the HC-130H extended-range model for the Aerospace Rescue and Recovery Service with a fold-out nose installation for the snatching of people or payloads from the ground. The JHC-130H model has further gear for aerial recovery of space capsules. A more advanced model, with special direction-finding receivers but without long-range tanks, is the HC-130N. The HC-130P model combines the mid-air retrieval capability with a tanking and air-refuelling function for helicopters.

This evergreen aircraft is by far the most important Air Force tactical airlifter and fulfils a host of secondary functions. Though civil and RAF versions have been stretched to match capacity to payload, this has not been done by the USAF. Production continues, and six H models were ordered for the AFRes and ANG in July 1981. New roles being studied by the Air Force include the C-130H-MP maritime patroller with offshore surveillance equipment, and the CAML (cargo aircraft minelayer) system using hydraulically powered pallets for rapid-sequence deployment of large sea mines. Should CAML be adopted, Air Force C-130s could fly minelaying missions for the Navy.

The Navy itself uses many C-130s, but was pipped to the post by the Marines who began in August 1957 with C-130As used in the tanker role. Subsequently the Marines bought 46 KC-130F and (so far) 14 KC-130R tankers with twin hosereels in wingtip pods. Among Navy versions are the EC-130G and EC-130Q Tacamo (special communications, especially for ballistic-missile submarines), DC-130 drone directors and LC-130F and R wheel/ski aircraft used mainly in Antarctica.

---

ramp/door, side paratroop doors, upper-surface roll/airbrake spoilers, four reversers, tape instruments, an all-weather landing system and advanced loading and positioning systems for pallets and other loads.

The first five C-141As were ordered in August 1961, at which time the requirement was for 132 aircraft, but following extremely rapid development and service introduction further orders were placed for a total of 285. Several of the first block were structurally modified to improve the ability of the floor to support the skids of a containerized Minuteman ICBM, a weight of 86,207lb (39,103kg). One of these aircraft set a world record in parachuting a single mass of 70,195lb (31,840kg). Standard loads included 10 regular 463L cargo pallets, 154 troops, 123 paratroops or 80 litter (stretcher) patients plus 16 medical attendants. Usable volume was 5,290 cu ft (150m³), not including the ramp. Service experience proved exemplary and in the Vietnam war C-141s, many of them specially equipped for medical missions and flown with extraordinary skill to ensure a smooth ride even through severe weather, maintained essentially a daily schedule on a 10,000-mile (16,000km) trip with full loads both ways.

It was this full-load experience which finally drove home the lesson that the C-141 could use more cubic capacity. Lockheed devised a cost/effective stretch which adds 'plugs' ahead of and behind the wing which extend the usable length by 23ft 4in (7.11m), increasing the usable volume (including the ramp) to 11,399cu ft (322.71m³). The extended aircraft, designated C-141B, carries 13 pallets or much larger numbers of personnel. It also incorporates an improved wing/body fairing which reduces drag and fuel burn per unit distance flown, while among other modifications the most prominent is a dorsal bulge aft of the flight deck housing a universal (boom or drogue) flight-refuelling receptacle. The first conversion, the YC-141B, was so successful that the Air Force decided to have Lockheed rework all the surviving aircraft (277), to give in effect the airlift ability of 90 additional aircraft with no extra fuel consumption.

In fact only 270 C-141B StarLifters were produced, the last being redelivered from Marietta on 29 June 1982. The entire rebuild programme was completed ahead of schedule and below cost. They are assigned to the

Above: This four-colour camouflage is one of several colour schemes which were investigated on large aircraft in 1980. There is no intention to depart at present from the standard all-grey colour of the MAC C-141Bs though some have white tops.

following MAWs: 60th at Travis, California; 63rd at Norton, California; 437th at Charleston, S Carolina; 438th at McGuire, NJ; 443rd at Altus, Oklahoma; and to part of the 314th TAW at Little Rock, Arkansas.

Lockheed P-3 Orion

P-3A, -3B and -3C with derivatives

Origin: Lockheed-California Co.
Type: Marine reconnaissance and anti-submarine, normally with flight crew of five and tactical crew of five; variants, see text.
Engines: Four Allison T56 single-shaft turboprops; (P-3A) T56-10W, 4,500ehp with water injection; (remainder) T56-14, 4,910ehp.
Dimensions: Span 99ft 8in (30.37m); length 116ft 10in (35.61m); height 33ft 8½in (10.29m); wing area 1,300sq ft (120.77m²).
Weights: Empty (typical B, C) 61,491lb (27,890kg); maximum loaded 142,000lb (64,410kg).
Performance: Maximum speed 473mph (761km/h); initial climb 1,950ft (594m)/min; service ceiling 28,300ft (8,625m); range 4,800 miles (7,725km).
Armament: Very varied load in bulged unpressurized weapon bay ahead of wing and on ten wing pylons; maximum internal load 7,252lb (3,290kg) can include two depth bombs, four Mk 44 torpedoes, 87 sonobuoys and many other sensing and marking devices; underwing load can include six 2,000lb (907kg) mines or various mixes of torpedoes, bombs, rockets or missiles. Maximum expendable load 20,000lb (9,071kg).
History: First flight (aerodynamic prototype) 19 August 1958; (YP-3A) 25 November 1959; (production P-3A) 15 April 1961; (P-3C) 18 September 1968.

Development: In August 1957 the US Navy issued a requirement for an "off the shelf" anti-submarine patrol aircraft derived from an established type, and this was met in April 1958 by Lockheed's proposal for a conversion of the Electra turboprop airliner. The third Electra was quickly modified as an aerodynamic prototype and deliveries of production P-3As began in August 1962. From the 110th aircraft the Deltic system was fitted with improved sensors, and after delivering 157 P-3As production switched to the P-3B with the more powerful Dash-14 engine which does not need a water/alcohol injection system. Lockheed supplied the US Navy with 124 of the B-model, surviving examples of which have been improved in various ways. By far the most important version is the P-3C, flown in 1968, which has largely new sensors and displays all linked by a digital computer. This soon became the definitive variant but has itself been the subject of successive Update programmes. From 1975 the P-3C Update introduced better navigation, sensor and data-processing capability. In 1976 Update II introduced an infra-red detection system in a chin turret, sonobuoy reference system and the capability to fire Harpoon missiles from wing pylons. A much more extensive revision was started in 1978 as Update III with completely altered ASW avionics, deliveries of this sub-type being due to start in April 1984. Deliveries of all P-3C versions reached 211 by 1983, with five per year expected through 1988. Rebuilds include WP-3A weather aircraft and various EP-3 Elint (electronic intelligence) aircraft serving with VQ-1 and -2.

Below: Pictured before delivery, this is a P-3C Update II of the 1977 period, which from 1984 will give way to the Update III.

Lockheed S-3 Viking

S-3A Viking, US-3A and S-3B

Origin: Lockheed-California Co.
Type: (S-3A, S-3B) four-seat carrier-based anti-submarine aircraft; (US-3A) carrier on-board delivery transport.
Engines: Two 9,275lb (4,207kg) General Electric TF34-400A two-shaft turbofans.
Dimensions: Span 68ft 8in (20.93m); length 53ft 4in (16.26m); height **22ft 9in (6.93m); wing area 598sq ft (55.55m²).**
Weights: Empty 26,600lb (12,065kg); normal loaded for carrier operation 42,500lb (19,277kg); maximum loaded 52,539lb (23,831kg).
Performance: Maximum speed 506mph (814km/h); initial climb, over 4,200ft (1,280m)/min; service ceiling, above 35,000ft (10,670m); combat range, more than 2,303 miles (3,705km); ferry range, more than 3,454 miles (5,558km).
Armament: Split internal weapon bays can house four Mk 46 torpedoes, four Mk 82 bombs, four various depth bombs or four mines; two wing pylons can carry single or triple ejectors for bombs, rocket pods, missiles, tanks or other stores.
History: First flight 21 January 1972; service delivery October 1973; operational use (VS-41) 20 February 1974; final delivery after 1980.

Development: Designed to replace the evergreen Grumman S-2, the S-3 is perhaps the most remarkable exercise in packaging in the history of aviation. It is also an example of an aircraft in which the operational equipment costs considerably more than the aircraft itself. Lockheed-California won the Navy competition in partnership with LTV (Vought) which makes the wing, engine pods, tail and F-8 type landing gear. To increase transit speed the refuelling probe, MAD tail boom, FLIR (forward-looking infra-red) and certain other sensors all retract, while the extremely modern specially designed APS-116 radar is within the nose. Equipment includes CAINS (carrier aircraft inertial navigation system), comprehensive sonobuoy dispensing and control systems, doppler, very extensive radio navaid and altitude systems, radar

warning and ECM systems, extensive communications, and a Univac digital processor to manage all tactical and navigation information. By the middle of 1978 production of the 187 S-3As for the US Navy had been completed, the bulk of these aircraft being deployed in the 13 carrier air groups embarked in large attack carriers as the standard ASW type. Three early Vikings have been modified to the US-3A COD (Carrier On-board Delivery) transport configuration with accommodation for 4,000lb (1,814kg) of cargo in two large underwing containers and six passengers and a little additional cargo in the fuselage. A redesigned large-body COD version has not been procured, neither has the impressive KS-3A tanker which, like the demonstrator US-3A, was evaluated in 1980. Nevertheless tooling exists for possible future procurement. Meanwhile in 1982-88 Lockheed is converting a planned 160 S-3As to S-3B standard with greatly augmented acoustic and radar processing capacity, expanded ESM (electronic support measures), a new APU (auxiliary power unit), new sonobuoy receiver and capability to fire the Harpoon anti-ship missile.

Below: Indistinguishable externally (from a distance) from the S-3B, these S-3As were photographed serving with VS-22 "Checkmates" from Cecil Field or embarked aboard USS Saratoga.

Lockheed SR-71

SR-71 A, B and C

Origin: Lockheed-California Co.
Type: A, strategic reconnaissance; B, C, trainer.
Powerplant: Two 32,500lb (14,742kg) thrust Pratt & Whitney J58-1 (JT11D-20B) continuous-bleed afterburning turbojets.
Dimensions: Span 55ft 7in (16.94m); length 107ft 5in (32.74m); wing area 1,800sq ft (167.2m²); height 18ft 6in (5.64m).
Weights: Empty, not disclosed, but about 65,000lb (29.5t); loaded 170,000lb (77,112kg).
Performance: Maximum speed (also maximum cruising speed), about 2,100mph (3,380km/h) at over 60,000ft (18.29km), world record speed over 15/25km course, 2,193mph (3,530km/h, Mach 3.31); maximum sustained height (also world record), 85,069ft (25,929m); range at 78,740ft (24km) at 1,983mph (3191km/h, Mach 3) on internal fuel, 2,982 miles (4,800km); corresponding endurance, 1h 30min; endurance at loiter speed, up to 7h.
Armament: None.
History: First flight (A-11) 26 April 1962; (SR-71A) 22 December 1964; service delivery, January 1966.

Development: Unbelievably, Lockheed and the Air Force succeeded in designing, building and completing the flight-test programme of these extremely large and noisy aircraft in total secrecy. President Johnson disclosed the existence of the basic A-11 design in February 1964. It was created by Lockheed's Advanced Development Projects team-–the so-called Skunk Works-–under vice-president C.L. 'Kelly' Johnson in 1959-61. The requirement was for a platform able to succeed the U-2 for clandestine reconnaissance, and as height was no longer sufficient protection, speed had to be added (which in turn translated into still greater height). Unprecedented engineering problems were encountered with the airframe (made principally from titanium and its alloys, never before used for primary structure), the propulsion system (which at cruising speed glows orange-white at the nozzles yet gets most of its thrust from the inlets) and even the hydraulic system (which uses completely new materials and techniques). Basic features included a modified delta wing with pronounced camber on the outer leading edges, extremely large lifting strakes extended forwards along the body and nacelles, twin inwards-canted pivoted fins above the nacelles, outboard ailerons, inboard elevators and main gears with three wheels side-by-side. The original A-11 shape also featured fixed ventral fins under the rear of the nacelles and a larger hinged central ventral fin.

The first three aircraft (60-6934/6) were built as YF-12A research interceptors, with a pressurized cockpit for a pilot and an air interception officer, Hughes ASG-18 pulse-doppler radar, side chines cut back to avoid the radome and provide lateral locations for two IR seekers, and tandem

Above: No American aircraft fly stranger nor less publicized missions than the SR-71s of 9th SRW; this one is being parked.

Below: Ship 61-7955 bears the snake emblem on its fins which shows it flew combat missions over Southeast Asia in 1967-73.

missile bays for (usually) eight AIM-47 AAMs. In 1969-72 two participated in a joint programme with NASA to investigate many aspects of flight at around Mach 3. These aircraft investigated surface finishes other than the normal bluish-black which resulted in the popular name of 'Blackbird' for all aircraft of this family.

It is believed that about 15 aircraft were delivered to the Air Force with a generally similar standard of build, though configured for the reconnaissance/strike role. Designated A-11, they could carry a centreline pod which could be a 1-megaton bomb but was usually a GTD-21 reconnaissance drone looking like a scaled-down single-engined A-11 and with cameras, IR and (variously, according to mission) other sensors in a bay behind the multi-shock centrebody nose inlet. Some dozens of these RPVs were delivered, painted the same heat-reflective black and with similar flight performance (engine has not been disclosed) but with rather shorter endurance. Those not consumed in missions (about 17) were stored at Davis-Monthan.

The A-11/GTD-21 held the fort until, in 1964, the definitive long-range

Above: Touchdown by an SR-71B trainer, with full left rudder (the entire tails move) and 40ft chute deployed.

recon/strike RS-71A came into service. (It was announced by President Johnson as the SR-71A and as he was never corrected the 'SR' designation became accepted.) This also can carry a 1-MT bomb pod or GTD-21 or derived RPV, but details of missions and payloads have not been disclosed. With an airframe and increased-capacity fuel system first flown on the fourth A-11 (designated YF-12C) it is longer, has no rear ventrals, optimized forward chines extending to the tip of the nose, and no missile bay but extremely comprehensive and in some cases unique reconnaissance systems for the surveillance of from 60,000 to 80,000 square miles (155,000 to 207,000km²) per hour. The backseater, with a separate clamshell canopy with inserted panes of heat-resistant glass, is the RSO, reconnaissance systems officer. Both crew wear Astronaut suits and follow pre-flight procedures based on those of space missions. The first SR-71A was assigned to a new unit, the 4,200th SRW, at Beale AFB, California, in 1966, which worked up the optimum operating procedures and techniques for best coverage, optimum fuel consumption, minimal signatures and precision navigation, burning special JP-7 fuel topped up in flight by KC-135Q tankers also based at Beale. To facilitate the demanding process of crew conversion to this extremely costly aircraft an operational trainer, the SR-71B, was purchased, at least two being slotted into the main batch of 29 (or more) which began at 61-7950. This has a raised instructor cockpit and dual pilot controls, and also includes the reconnaissance systems for RSO training.

After the first crews had qualified as fully operational, in 1971, the parent wing was restyled the 9th SRW, with two squadrons. This has ever since operated in a clandestine manner, rarely more than two aircraft being despatched to any overseas theatre and missions normally being flown by single aircraft. It is not known to what extent subsonic cruise is used; in the normal high-speed regime the skin temperature rises from -49°C to 550/595°C, and the fuel serves as the heat sink and rises to a temperature of about 320°C before reaching the engines. At least one SR-71C was produced as an SR-71A rebuild, following loss of an SR-71B. It has been estimated that the SR-71As seldom fly more than 200 hours per year, mainly on training exercises. No recent estimate has been published of their vulnerability.

Lockheed TR-1

U-2A, B, C, CT, D, R, WU-2 family and TR-1A & B.

Origin: Lockheed-California Co.

Engine: One Pratt & Whitney unaugmented turbojet, (A and some derivatives) 11,200lb (5,080kg) thrust J57-13A or -37A, (most other U-2) versions, one 17,000lb (7,711kg) thrust J75-13, (TR-1) 17,000lb (7,711kg) J75-13B.

Dimensions: Span (A,B,C,D,CT) 80ft 0in (24,38m), (R, WU-2C, TR-1), 103ft 0in (31.39m)ength (typical of early versions) 49ft 7in (15.1m), (R,TR) 63ft 0in (19.2m); wing area (early) 565sq ft (52.49m²), (R, TR) 1,000sq ft (92.9m²).

Weights: Empty (A) 9,920lb (4,500kg), (B,C,CT,D) typically 11,700lb (5,305kg), (R) 14,990lb (6,800kg), (TR) about 16,000lb (7,258kg); loaded (A) 14,800lb (6,713kg), (B,C,CT,D, clean) typically 16,000lb (7,258kg), (with 89 US gal wing tanks) 17,270lb (7,833kg), (R) 29,000lb (13,154kg), (TR) 40,000lb (18,144kg).

Performance: Maximum speed (A) 494mph (795km/h), (B,C,CT,D) 528mph (850km/h), (R) about 510mph (821km/h), (TR) probably about 495mph (797km/h); maximum cruising speed (most) 460mph (740km/h), (TR) 430mph (692km/h); operational ceiling (A) 70,000ft (21.34km), (B,C, CT, D) 85,000ft (25.9km), (R,TR) about 90,000ft (27.43km); maximum range (A) 2,200 miles (3,540km), (B,C,CT,D) 3,000 miles (4,830km), (R) about 3,500 miles (5,833km), (TR) about 4,000 miles (6,437km); endurance on internal fuel (A) 5½ h, (B,C,CT,D) 6½ h, (R) 7½ h, (TR) 12 h.

Armament: None.

History: First flight (A) 1 August 1955; service delivery February 1956; operational service, June 1957; (TR) September 1981.

Development: First of the two families of clandestine surveillance aircraft produced by Lockheed's 'Skunk Works' under the brilliant engineering leadership of C.L. 'Kelly' Johnson, the U-2 was conceived in spring 1954 to meet an unannounced joint USAF/CIA requirement for a reconnaissance and research aircraft to cruise at the highest attainable altitudes. The entire programme was cloaked in secrecy, test flying (under Tony LeVier) took place at remote Watertown Strip, Nevada, and no announcement was made of delivery to the Air Force of 56-675 and -676, the two prototypes. The original order comprised 48 single-seaters and five tandem-seat aircraft, initially the back-seater being an observer or systems operator. The operating unit was styled Weather Reconnaissance Squadron, Provisional (1st) and soon moved to Atsugi AB, Japan, while the WRS,P (2nd) moved to Wiesbaden, Germany, with basing also at Lakenheath, England. The WRS,P(3rd) remained at Edwards to develop techniques and handle research.

Intense interest in the aircraft, grey and without markings, prompted an announcement that they were NASA research aircraft, with Utility designation

Below: Because of its much greater weight the TR-1 is slightly less difficult to land than early U-2s but it still needs great skill and concentration. It comes to rest on a wingtip.

U-2, but after numerous unmolested missions over the Soviet Union, China and other territories, one of the CIA aircraft was shot down near Sverdlovsk on 1 May 1960. Future missions were flown by USAF pilots in uniform, with USAF markings on the aircraft. Several more J75-powered aircraft were shot down over China and Cuba, and attrition was also fairly high from accidents, because the U-2 is possibly the most difficult of all modern aircraft to fly. Features include an all-metal airframe of sailplane-like qualities, with a lightly loaded and extremely flexible wing, tandem bicycle landing gears, outrigger twin-wheel units jettisoned on takeoff (the landing tipping on to a downturned wingtip), an unpressurized cockpit with UV-protected sliding canopy of F-104 type, special low-volatility fuel, and large flaps, airbrakes and braking parachute.

McDonnell Douglas A-4 Skyhawk

A-4A to A-4S and TA-4 series

Origin: Douglas Aircraft Co, El Segundo (now division of McDonnell Douglas, Long Beach).

Type: Single-seat attack bomber; TA, dual-control trainer.

Engine: (B, C, L, P, Q, S) one 7,700lb (3,493kg) thrust Wright J65-16A single-shaft turbojet (US Sapphire); (E, J) 8,500lb (3,856kg) Pratt & Whitney J52-6 two-shaft turbojet; (F, G, H, K) 9,300lb (4,218kg) J52-8A; (M, N) 11,200lb (5,080kg) J52-408A.

Dimensions: Span 27ft 6in (8.38m);length (A)39ft 1in; (B) 39ft 6in (42ft 10¾in over FR probe); (E, F, G, H, K, L, P, Q, S) 40ft 1½in (12.22m); (M, N) 40ft 3¼in (12.27m); (TA series, excluding probe) 42ft 7¼in (12.98m); height 15ft (4.57m); (early single-seaters 15ft 2in, TA series 15ft 3in).

Weights: Empty (A) 7,700lb; (E) 9,284lb; (typical modern single-seat, eg M) 10,465lb (4,747kg); (TA-4F) 10,602lb (4,809kg); maximum loaded (A) 17,000lb; (B) 22,000lb; (all others, shipboard) 24,500lb (11,113kg); (land-based) 27,420lb (12,437kg).

Performance: Maximum speed (clean) (B) 676mph; (E) 685mph; (M) 670mph (1,078km/h) (TA-4F) 675mph; maximum speed (4,000lb 1,814kg bomb load) (F) 593mph; (M) 645mph; initial climb (F) 5,620ft (1,713m)/ min; (M) 8,440ft (2,572m)/min; service ceiling (all, clean) about 49,000ft (14,935m); range (clean, or with 4,000lb weapons and max fuel, all late versions) about 920 miles (1,480km); maximum range (M) 2,055 miles (3,307km).

Armament: Standard on most versions, two 20mm Mk 12 cannon, each with 200 rounds; (H, N, and optional on other export versions) two 30mm DEFA 553, each with 150 rounds. Pylons under fuselage and wings for total ordnance load of (A, B, C) 5,000lb (2,268kg); (E, F, G, H, K, L, P, Q, S) 8,200lb (3,720kg); (M, N) 9,155lb (4,153kg).

History: First flight (XA4D-1) 22 June 1954; (A-4A) 14 August 1954; squadron delivery October 1956; (A-4C) August 1959; (A-4E) July 1961; (A-4F) August 1966; (A-4M) April 1970; (A-4N) June 1972; first of TA series (TA-4E) June 1965.

Development: Most expert opinion in the US Navy refused to believe the claim of Ed Heinemann, chief engineer of what was then Douglas El Segundo, that he could build a jet attack bomber weighing half the 30,000lb specified by the Navy. The first Skyhawk, nicknamed "Heinemann's Hot

Rod", not only flew but gained a world record by flying a 500km circuit at over 695mph. Today some 30 years later, greatly developed versions are still in use. These late versions do weigh close to 30,000lb, but only because the basic design has been improved with more powerful engines, increased fuel capacity and much heavier weapon load. The wing was made in a single unit, forming an integral fuel tank and so small it did not need to fold. Hundreds of Skyhawks have served aboard carriers, but in the US involvement in SE Asia "The Scooter" (as it was affectionately known) flew many kinds of mission from land bases. In early versions the emphasis was on improving range and load and the addition of all-weather avionics. The F model introduced the dorsal hump containing additional avionics, and the M, the so-called Skyhawk II, marked a major increase in mission effectiveness. Most of the TA-4 trainers closely resembled the corresponding single-seater, but the TA-4J and certain other models have simplified avionics and are used not only for advanced pilot training but also by the "Top Gun" and similar fighter-pilot training units for dissimilar aircraft combat training. Though production was completed in 1979 after 26 unbroken years, with deliveries amounting to 2,405 attack models and 555 two-seaters, updating programmes continue to improve survivors in Navy and Marine Corps service. There is also a major rebuild programme which since 1980 has given the Marines 23 two-seat TA-4F trainers rebuilt as OA-4M FAC (Forward Air Control) platforms with avionics basically as in the A-4M and the rear canopy section faired into the "camel hump".

Above: The first TR-1A single-seater, No 80-1066, pictured at Palmdale on roll-out in July 1981. By early 1983 two had reached RAF Alconbury in England with two more imminently expected.

From 1959 the J75 engine was installed, and with the U-2C the inlets were splayed out at the front, the U-2D being the original two-seat version and the U-2CT (conversion trainer) being one of at least six rebuilds, in this example as a dual-control pilot trainer with the instructor seated at an upper level. Most CTs have been stationed at the Air Force Flight Test Center and Test Pilot School, both at Edwards. The AFFTC also uses several other versions, including D variants with special instrumentation, dorsal or ventral inlets for sampling, and various external payloads, with a variety of black, white and other paint schemes. Both C and D models have large dorsal 'doghouse' fairings for sampling, sensing or avionic equipment.

Because of high attrition the line was reopened in 1968 with 12 considerably larger aircraft styled U-2R (68-10329 to 10340). While most earlier models could carry 80 US gal (336lit) tanks on the leading edge, the R was supplied with large wing pods permanently installed and accommodating various payloads as well as 105 US gal (398lit) fuel. Wet wings increased internal capacity, and the R also introduced a stretched airframe able to accommodate all necessary fuel and equipment internally. Front and rear main gears were moved closer together and the rear fuselage was formed into a bulged upper platform carrying the tailplane. All known U-2R aircraft have been matt black, serving with various overseas commands.

The latest variant, the TR-1, is basically a further updated U-2R with ASARS (Advanced Synthetic-Aperture Radar System), in the form of the UPD-X side-looking airborne radar, and with dramatically increased integral-tank fuel capacity, which results in very much higher gross weight. A single-seater, like the R, the TR-1A carries extensive new avionics in its pods, as well

as much more comprehensive ECM. Mission equipment is also carried in the nose, in the Q-bay behind the cockpit and between the inlet ducts. Because of the long endurance the Astronaut-suited pilot has special facilities for his personal comfort and for taking warm food. The first batch comprised two TR-1As (80-1061 and 1062) and a third aircraft (1063) which was actually first to be delivered, on 10 June 1981, via the Air Force to NASA with designation ER-2 for earth-resource missions. Next followed three more TR-1As and a two-seat TR-1B, the eventual fleet expected to number 33 As and two Bs. Ten of the single-seaters are to be allocated to the PLSS (Precision Location Strike System) mission for pinpointing and destroying electronic emitters far into hostile territory. Of the remaining 25 aircraft 18 are to be based at RAF Alconbury, England, where operations began under SAC control in early 1983. Forward operating locations in Germany and elsewhere will extend mission endurance over Warsaw Pact frontiers.

Below: Externally almost identical to a TR-1A, this is actually a U-2R (No 68-10329) which has totally different mission equipment.

Below: Much smaller, and half the weight of a TR-1, this U-2L was one of several converted from U-2B configuration to carry out upper-atmosphere radiation measurements (mainly following foreign nuclear-weapon testing). Several are still in use.

Left: An A-4M Skyhawk II of Marine Corps attack squadron VMA-214 seen on deployment from its base at El Toro to weapons practice at Yuma, Arizona. Loads comprised tank, rocket pods and ECM pods. Marine A-4s are shortly to be replaced by Harrier IIs.

Above: One of the standard A-4 weapons continues to be the AGM-45 Shrike anti-radar missile, though of course VA-55 of the Navy no longer flies the A-4. Considerable numbers of seven major versions are now stored and unlikely to be needed.

McDonnell Douglas/
BAe AV-8B Harrier II

AV-8B

Origin: McDonnell Douglas (St Louis), USA, and BAe, UK.
Type: Single-seat attack and close support aircraft.
Engine: One 22,000lb (9,979kg) Pratt & Whitney F402-RR-406 (Pegasus 11-21) vectored-thrust turbofan.
Dimensions: Span 30ft 4in (9.25m); length 46ft 4in (14.12m); height 11ft 7¾in (3.55m); wing area 230sq ft (21.37m²).
Weights: Empty 12,750lb (5,783kg); loaded (VTO) 19,550lb (8,867kg); maximum 29,750lb (13,494kg).
Performance: Maximum speed (clean, SL) 673mph (1,083km/h); takeoff run at max weight 1,200ft (366m); combat radius (seven Mk 82 Snakeye bombs and tanks) 748 miles (1,204km); ferry range 3,310 miles (5,328km).
Armament: One 25mm GAU-12/U gun with 300 rounds; seven external pylons for maximum load of 7,000lb (3,175kg) for VTO or 17,000lb (7,711kg) for rolling takeoff, including 16 GP bombs, 10 Paveway weapons, 2/4 AIM-9L Sidewinders or AGM-65A or E Mavericks and very wide range of other stores including ALQ-164 ECM pod on centreline.
History: First flight (YAV-8B) 9 November 1978, (AV-8B) 5 November 1981; service delivery October 1983.

Development: The British government's shortsighted withdrawal from a common programme of development of an Advanced Harrier in 1973 resulted in 1981 in the RAF having to accept the McDonnell Douglas-developed AV-8B, which accordingly was then permitted to go ahead into FSD (full-scale development) after having for three years lain in the doldrums while US money was poured into the same company's F/A-18A. Though Rolls-Royce could have done many things to increase power of the engine there was no money for this purpose, so the F402 (US designation) will have features aimed at increasing life and reducing costs. It does, however, have long zero-scarf (cut square) front nozzles which increase lift in the VTO mode, and the inlets are redesigned for higher thrust and efficiency. The main airframe change is a totally new long-span wing, with deep super-critical section and less sweep, which with other changes increases internal fuel by more than 50 per cent. Very large flaps are lowered in the VTO mode and combined with lift-improvement devices under the fuselage and the new nozzles result in more than 7,500lb (3,402kg) more VTO lift and even greater gains in rolling takeoffs. Extra pylons handle the greater weapon loads possible, and combined with the increased fuel capacity result in payload/range figures improved by roughly 100 per cent over the earlier AV-8A or C. Further changes include a raised cockpit and canopy (not the same as in the British Sea Harrier), retractable inflight-refuelling probe, Stencel seat, LERXs (leading-edge root extensions to enhance inflight agility) and greatly updated avionics including the Angle Rate Bombing System, advanced HUD and cockpit displays, inertial system and IBM digital computer. British Aerospace has 40 per cent of the main programme of 336 aircraft for the US Marine Corps inventory, which by 1989 are expected to replace the AV-8C in VMA(T)-203, VMA-231 and 542. The Marines are also expected to buy 18 dual TAV-8B trainers, and further sales are likely for other missions and possibly for the Navy or other US services.

Right: Now in full production, the AV-8B Harrier II, seen here fitted with the definitive wing with LERX, is to be supplemented by the TAV-8B dual conversion trainer.

McDonnell Douglas F-4
Phantom II

F-4A to F-4S, RF-4 and QF-4

Origin: McDonnell Aircraft, division of McDonnell Douglas Corp, St Louis.
Type: Originally carrier-based all-weather interceptor, now all-weather multi-role fighter for ship or land operation; (RF) all-weather multisensor reconnaissance; (QF) RPV; (F-4G) defence-suppression aircraft.
Engines: (B) two 17,000lb (7,711kg) thrust General Electric J79-8 single-shaft turbojets with afterburner; (C, D) 17,000lb J79-15; (E, F, G) 17,900lb (8,120kg) J79-17; (J, N, S) 17,900lb J79-10.
Dimensions: Span 38ft 5in (11.7m); length (B, C, D, J, N, S) 58ft 3in (17.76m); (E, F and all RF versions) 62ft 11in or 63ft (19.2m); (K, M) 57ft 7in (17.55m); height (all) 16ft 3in (4.96m).
Weights: Empty (B) 28,000lb (12,700kg), (C, D, J) 28,200lb (12,792kg), (RF) 29,300lb (13,290kg), (E) 30,328lb (13,757kg), (G) 30,900lb (14,016kg); maximum (B) 54,600lb (24,767kg); (C, D, J, RF) 58,000lb (26,309kg), (E, G) 60,360lb (27,379kg).
Performance: Maximum speed with Sparrow missiles only (low) 910mph (1,464km/h, Mach 1.19), (high) 1,500mph (2,414km/h, Mach 2.27); initial climb, typically 28,000ft (8,534m)/min; service ceiling, over 60,000ft (19,685m) with J79 engines, 60,000ft with Spey; range on internal fuel (no weapons) about 1,750 miles (2,817km); ferry range with external fuel, typically 2,300 miles (3,700km) (E and variants, 2,600 miles (4,184km).
Armament: (All versions except RF, QF which have no armament) four AIM-7 Sparrow air-to-air missiles recessed under fuselage; inner wing pylons can carry two more AIM-7 or four AIM-9 Sidewinder missiles; in addition all E versions except RF have internal 20mm M-61 multi-barrel gun, and virtually all versions can carry the same gun in external centreline pod; all except RF, QF have centreline and four wing pylons for tanks, bombs or other stores to total weight of 16,000lb (7,257kg).
History: First flight (XF4H-1) 27 May 1958; service delivery (F-4A) February 1960 (carrier trials), February 1961 (inventory); first flight (Air Force F-4C) 27 May 1963; (F-4E) 30 June 1967; (EF-4E) 1976; final delivery March 1979.

Development: McDonnell designed the greatest fighter of the postwar era as a company venture to meet anticipated future needs. Planned as an attack aircraft with four 20mm guns, it was changed into a very advanced gunless all-weather interceptor with advanced radar and missile armament. In this form it entered service as the F-4A, soon followed by the F-4B used in large numbers (635) by the US Navy and Marine Corps, with Westing-house APQ-72 radar, IR detector in a small fairing under the nose, and many weapon options. Pilot and radar intercept officer sit in tandem and the aircraft has blown flaps and extremely comprehensive combat equipment. A level Mach number of 2.6 was achieved and many world records were set for speed, altitude and rate of climb. Not replaced by the abandoned F-111B, the carrier-based Phantom continued in production for 19 years through the F-4G with digital communications, F-4J with AWG-10 pulse-doppler radar, drooping ailerons, slatted tail and increased power, and the N (rebuilt B). In 1973-5 Navy facilities delivered 178 F-4Ns with completely revised avionics and strengthened airframe, as well as conversions of the original F-4A to TF-4A trainers and F-4Bs to QF-4B remotely piloted drones, since used in substantial numbers as missile targets and for other purposes. The F-4Gs were returned to normal (N) standard and the designation was later used for a totally different USAF model. The final Navy/Marines variant is the F-4S, 265 of which were produced in-house by rebuilding F-4Js with

improved avionics, strengthened structure (including completely new outer wings with slats) and a total electrical rewiring.

These outstanding aircraft outperformed and outnumbered all other US combat aircraft of the 1960s. Vastly increased production, rising to a remarkable 75 per month in 1967, stemmed not only from the Vietnam war but also because the Air Force recognized that the F-4 beat even the specialist land-based types at their own missions, and after prolonged study decided to buy the basic F-4B version with minimal changes. The original Air Force designation of F-110 Spectre was changed to F-4C Phantom II under the unified 1962 system, the F-4C being a minimum-change version of the Navy B and preceded (from 24 January 1962) by the loan to TAC of 30 B models ex-Navy.

After buying 583 F-4Cs with dual controls, a boom receptacle, Dash-15 engines with cartridge starters, larger tyres and increased-capacity brakes, inertial navigation and improved weapon aiming, the Air Force procured 793 of the F-4D model which was tailored to its own land-based missions, with APQ-109 radar, ASG-22 servoed sight, ASQ-91 weapon-release computer for nuclear LABS manoeuvres, improved inertial system and 30-kVA alternators. Visually, many Ds could be distinguished by removal of the AAA-4 IR detector in a pod under the radar, always present on the C. Next came the extremely sophisticated RF-4C multi-sensor reconnaissance aircraft, a major rebuild in a programme which preceded the D by two years and was the first Air Force variant to be authorized. Designed to supplement and then replace the RF-101 family the RF-4C was unarmed but was modified to carry a battery of forward-looking and oblique cameras, IR linescan, SLAR (side-looking airborne radar) and a small forward oblique mapping radar, as well as more than 20 auxiliary fits including photo flash/flare cartridges in the top of the rear fuselage, special ECM and HF shunt aerials built into the fin behind the leading edge on each side. TAC purchased 505 of this model in 1964-73.

All these variants were very heavily engaged in the war in SE Asia in 1966-73, where political rules combined with other problems to reduce their air-combat performance. Prolonged call for an internal gun resulted in the F-4E, which had the most powerful J79 engine to permit the flight performance to be maintained despite adding weight at both ends. In the nose was the new solid-state APQ-120 radar and the M61 gun, slanting down on

Above: One of the famed USAF units still flying the F-4E is the 4th Tactical Fighter Wing based at Seymour Johnson AFB, North Carolina, whose badge appears on the inlet (with TAC badge on fin). The 4th has dual-base commitments to NATO in Europe.

the ventral centreline with the 6 o'clock firing barrel near-horizontal, and at the rear was a new (No 7) fuel cell giving enhanced range. The first E was delivered to TAC on 3 October 1967, about three months after first flight, and a total of 949 in all were supplied to maintain the F-4 as leading TAC aircraft with an average of 16 wings equipped throughout the period 1967/77. From 1972 all Es were rebuilt with a slatted leading edge, replacing the previous blown droop which permitted much tighter accelerative manoeuvres to be made, especially at high weights, without stall/spin accidents of the kind which had caused many losses in Vietnam.

The final Air Force variant is the F-4G, the standard Advanced Wild Weasel platform replacing the F-105F and G which pioneered Wild Weasel missions in the late 1960s. The name covers all dedicated EW and anti-SAM missions in which specially equipped electronic aircraft hunt down hostile SAM installations (using radar for lock-on, tracking or missile guidance) and destroy them before or during an attack by other friendly aircraft on nearby targets. The F-4G (the same designation was used previously for modified F-4Bs of the Navy) is a rebuild of late-model F-4E (F-4E-42 through -45) fighters, and has almost the same airframe. It is the successor to the EF-4C, two squadrons of which were fielded by TAC from 1968 and which demonstrated excellent performance with a simpler system. In the F-4G the main EW system is the AN/APR-38, which provides very comprehensive radar homing and warning and uses no fewer than 52 special aerials, of which the most obvious are pods facing forward under the nose (replacing the gun) and facing to the rear at the top of the vertical tail. The system is governed by a Texas Instruments reprogrammable software routine which thus keeps up to date on all known hostile emitters. Offensive weapons normally comprise triple AGM-65 EO-guided Mavericks on each inboard pylon plus a Shrike on each outer pylon; alternatively weapons can include the big Standard ARM (Anti-Radiation Missile), AGM-88 HARM (High-speed ARM) or various other precision air/ground weapons. A Westinghouse ALQ-119 jammer pod is fitted in the left front missile recess, the other three recesses carrying Sparrow AAMs for self-protection. Another change is to fit the F-15 type centreline tank which can take 5g when full with 600 US gal (2,271lit). The G total is 116 aircraft.

Left: A Maverick missile can be seen on this F-4G Advanced Wild Weasel of the 35th Tac Fighter Wing based at George AFB, Ca. Camouflage is the standard tan/dark green/medium green.

Below: ALQ-119(V)8 ECM pods nestle under the fuselages of these F-4Es departing on a mission in Exercise Team Spirit '82.

McDonnell Douglas F-15 Eagle

F-15A,B,C,D and E

Origin: McDonnell Aircraft Company, St Louis, Missouri.
Type: Air-superiority fighter with secondary attack role.
Powerplant: Two 23,930lb (10,855kg) thrust Pratt & Whitney F100-100 afterburning turbofans.
Dimensions: Span 42ft 9¾in (13.05m); length (all) 63ft 9in (19.43m); wing area 608sq ft (56.5m²); height 18ft 5½in (5.63m).
Weights: Empty (basic equipped) 28,000lb (12.7t); loaded (interception mission, max internal fuel plus four AIM-7, F-15A) 41,500lb (18,824kg), (C) 44,500lb (20,185kg); maximum with max external load (A) 56,500lb (25,628kg), (C) 68,000lb (30,845kg).
Performance: Maximum speed (over 36,000ft/10 973m with no external load except four AIM-7), 1,653mph (2,660km/h, Mach 2.5); with max external load or at low level, not published; initial climb (clean) over 50,000ft (15.24km)/min, (max wt) 29,000ft (8.8km)/min; service ceiling 65,000ft (19.8km); takeoff run (clean) 900ft (274m); landing run (clean, without brake chute) 2,500ft (762m); ferry range with three external tanks, over 2,878 miles (4,631km), (with Fast packs also) over 3,450 miles (5,560km).
Armament: One 20mm M61A-1 gun with 940 rounds, four AIM-7F (later AMRAAM) fitting against fuselage, four AIM-9L (later Asraam) on flanks of wing pylons, total additional ordnance load 16,000lb (7,257kg) on five stations (two each wing, one centreline).
History: First flight (A) 27 July 1972, (B) 7 July 1973; service delivery (Cat II test) March 1974, (inventory) November 1974.
Development: Recognizing its urgent need for a superior long-range air-combat fighter the Air Force requested development funds in 1965 and issued an RFP in September 1968 for the FX, the McDonnell proposal being selected in late 1969, with the F100 engine and Hughes APG-63 radar following in 1970. Inevitably the demand for long range resulted in a large aircraft, the wing having to be so large to meet the manoeuvre requirement that it has a fixed leading edge and plain unblown trailing-edge flaps. Two of the extremely powerful engines were needed to achieve the desired ratio of thrust/weight, which near sea level in the clean condition exceeds unity. The inlet ducts form the walls of the broad fuselage, with plain vertical rectangular inlets giving external compression from the forward-raked upper lip and with the entire inlet pivoted at the top and positioned at the optimum angle for each flight regime. The upper wall of the inlet forms a variable ramp, and the lower edge of the fuselage is tailored to snug fitting of the four medium-range AAMs. The gun is in the bulged strake at the root of the right wing, drawing ammunition from a tank inboard of the duct. There is

no fuel between the engines but abundant room in the integral-tank inner wing and between the ducts for 11,600lb (5,260kg, 1,739 US gal, 6,592lit), and three 600 US gal (2,270lit) drop tanks can be carried each stressed to 5g manoeuvres when full. Roll is by ailerons only at low speeds, the dogtoothed slab tailplanes taking over entirely at over Mach 1, together with the twin rudders, which are vertical.

Avionics and flight/weapon control systems are typical of the 1970 period, with a flat-plate scanner pulse-doppler radar, vertical situation display presenting ADI (attitude/director indicator), radar and EO information on one picture, a HUD, INS and central digital computer. In its integral ECM/IFF subsystems the F-15 was far better than most Western fighters, with Loral radar warning (with front/rear aerials on the left fin tip), Northrop ALQ-135 internal counter measures system, Magnavox EW warning set and Hazeltine APX-76 IFF with Litton reply-evaluator. High-power jammers, however, must still be hung externally, any of various Westinghouse

Above: Dive bombing F-15B which has been used for many trials and has served as the prototype Enhanced Tactical Fighter.

Left: Inspection of the Hughes multimode pulse-doppler radar type APG-63, in one of the first block of F-15A aircraft. For dogfighting the radar acquires target on the Head-up Display.

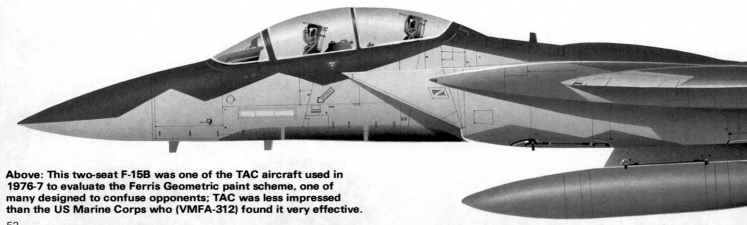

Above: This two-seat F-15B was one of the TAC aircraft used in 1976-7 to evaluate the Ferris Geometric paint scheme, one of many designed to confuse opponents; TAC was less impressed than the US Marine Corps who (VMFA-312) found it very effective.

pods normally occupying an outer wing pylon. The APG-63 offered a fantastic increase in ability to detect and track low-flying targets, and to display only features of interest to the pilot. Another advance was Hotas (Hands On Throttle and Stick) technology in the cockpit which dramatically improved dogfight performance. Though it was, and remains, concerned at the price, the Air Force got in the F-15A everything it was looking for and in 1973 announced a force of 729 aircraft including a proportion of tandem dual-control F-15B operational trainers.

Production at St Louis has been running at 90 to 144 aircraft per year, with 815 delivered by the time this book appears. Recipient units began with TAC's 57th TTW at Nellis, 58th TTW at Luke, 1st TFW at Langley, 36th TFW at Bitburg (Germany), 49th TFW at Holloman, 33rd TFW at Eglin, 32nd TFS at Camp New Amsterdam (Netherlands) and 18th TFW at Kadena (Okinawa). Some of these units have received the current production variants, the F-15C and two-seat F-15D. These have a vital electronic modification in a reprogrammable signal processor, giving instant ability to switch from one locked-on target to another, to keep looking whilst already locked to one target, to switch between air and ground targets and, by virtue of an increase in memory from 24K to 96K (96,000 'words'), to go into a high-resolution mode giving the ability to pick one target from a tight formation even at near the limit of radar range. To some extent the latter capability will remain not fully realized until a later medium-range AAM is used (the Air Force has studied the Navy AIM-54 Phoenix but not adopted it). The British Sky Flash would give a major improvement now, especially in severe jamming, but again has not been adopted. The C and D also have 2,000lb (907kg) of additional internal fuel and can carry the Fast (Fuel and sensor, tactical) packs cunningly devised by McDonnell to fit flush along the sides of the fuselage. These actually reduce subsonic drag and offer far less

Above: Start of peel-off manoeuvre by fully armed F-15As of the 32nd Tactical Fighter Wing from Camp New Amsterdam, Netherlands. The 32nd has won several proficiency awards.

Below: There are actually three F-15As in this photograph, which was taken from the back seat of an F-15B. Their unit is the 405th Tactical Training Wing at Luke AFB, near Phoenix, Arizona.

supersonic drag than the drop tanks whilst adding a further 9,750lb (4,422kg) fuel, or an assortment of sensors (cameras, FLIR, EO, LLTV or laser designator) or a mix of fuel and sensors.

In the second half of 1981 the F-15C re-equipped the 48th FIS at Langley, previously an F-106A unit in now-defunct Adcom, and the Air Force is now procuring aircraft beyond the original 729 force level, partly in order to replace the aged F-106 in CONUS defence. For the future, while one variant of F-15 has been subjected to prolonged study as the USAF's Asat (Anti-satellite) aircraft, firing a large air/space missile based on a SRAM motor followed by an Altair II carrying a nuclear warhead, prolonged testing and demonstration of a company-funded Strike Eagle has now led to the F-15E which may be on order by the time this book appears. This could serve as the Enhanced Tactical Fighter to replace the F-111 (the alternative being the Panavia Tornado) and also as the Advanced Wild Weasel (with far greater capability than the F-4G). The key is the SAR (synthetic-aperture radar) built into the APG-63, which very greatly improves resolution of fine detail against even distant ground targets. With a Pave Tack (FLIR/laser) pod the backseater in the two-seat F-15E can handle what are considered to be the best tactical navigation/target/weapon avionics in the world (apart from the strictly comparable Tornado). External weapon carriage is increased to 24,000lb (10,885kg), including laser-guided and anti-radiation weapons, Harpoon anti-ship missiles, dispensers and other stores. Whether the large existing F-15 force can eventually be brought up to this impressive standard is doubtful. In 1982 the 21st TFW in Alaska converted to the F-15C/D, and in 1983 the 1st TFW (Rapid Deployment Force) had converted to the C/D and was receiving the first Fast packs. The F-15E was engaged in a flyoff against the F-16XL; discounting the possible 400 of this version the USAF is expected to receive 1,395 Eagles by 1995, excluding the 20 development aircraft.

McDonnell Douglas
F/A-18 Hornet

F/A-18A, TF/A-18A and RF-18

Origin: McDonnell Douglas (St Louis); Northrop is principal subcontractor.
Type: Single-seat carrier-based strike fighter, (TF) combat-capable dual trainer, (RF) unarmed recon.
Engines: Two GE F404-400 augmented low-ratio turbofans (bypass turbojets) each "in 16,000lb (7,257kg) class".
Dimensions: Span (basic) 37ft 6in (11.43m), (over AAMs) 40ft 4¾in (12.31m); length 56ft 0in (17.07m); height 15ft 3½in (4.66m); wing area 400sq ft (37.16m²).
Weights: Empty 22,460lb (10,188kg); loaded (fighter) 33,585lb (15,234kg), (attack) 48,253lb (21,887kg).
Performance: Maximum speed (hi, clean) 1,200mph (1,931km/h, Mach 1.82); combat ceiling about 50,000ft (15km); combat radius (fighter, hi) 460 miles (740km), (attack, three tanks) 633 miles (1,019km).
Armament: M61A-1 20mm gun with 570 rounds; nine external pylons for total load of up to 17,000lb (7,711kg) including all normal Navy/Marines bombs, rockets, ASMs, 300US gal (1,136lit) tanks, AIM-9 and AIM-7 (later Amraam) AAMs, laser spot tracker, forward-looking infra-red and ECM pods.
History: First flight (YF-17) 9 June 1974, (first of 11 prototype F-18s) 18 November 1978; production delivery (for evaluation) May 1980.

Development: In 1974 the Navy was instructed by Congress to discontinue its new-design VFAX project for a low-cost lightweight fighter and instead study derivatives of the USAF YF-16 or YF-17. Called NACF (Navy Air Combat Fighter), the best submission turned out to be the Hornet proposed by McDonnell Douglas on the basis of the Northrop YF-17. Compared with the latter it has a larger wing, wider fuselage with much greater fuel capacity, bypass engines of increased thrust, heavier and more diverse weapon loads, and carrier features including folding wings and landing gear stressed for 24ft (7.32m)/s rate of descent and nose-tow catapult launch. The nose is enlarged to house the Hughes APG-65 liquid-cooled multimode digital radar able to track ten targets and display eight, and with illumination features for Sparrow or Amraam missiles. The gun is mounted in the upper part of the nose immediately behind the radar. The single-seat cockpit is more conventional than that of the F-16 but has extremely advanced displays. From the start severe numerical requirements for ease of maintenance had to be met, despite the dense packaging of the entire aircraft.

Originally it was planned to develop an F-18A fighter and an A-18 attack aircraft for the Marines, but eventually the differences were whittled away until a single standard was reached with the unique dual-role designation F/A-18A. This has been developed to replace the F-4 in the interceptor role and the A-4 and A-7 in the attack mission. The TF/A-18A has a rear instructor cockpit, and retains weapon capability but with about 6 per cent less internal

Above: Four F-18A Hornets of the US Navy's Air Test and Development Squadron VX-4 at Point Mugu.

Right: Fourth prototype of the F/A-18A, shown on level bombing trials with Mk 83 bombs carried in pairs.

fuel. The RF-18 reconnaissance version, first tested in late 1982, has a large camera/IR sensor package installed in the nose, the gun being removed; it can be identified by a ventral bulge. This model had not been ordered when this book went to press, but could be produced by field conversion if the standard aircraft were suitably modified for this additional role.

Development was swift but marked by several major problems which, combined with inevitable inflation, caused very severe escalation in price. The 11 development aircraft were all flying by March 1980. Eventually the more difficult problems, such as inadequate rate of roll, were overcome (the wing finally emerged with ailerons extending to the tips and with a full-span hinged leading edge without the dogtooth discontinuities of the early aircraft). The first nine production Hornets were funded in fiscal year 1979, 25 in 1980, 60 in 1981, 63 in 1982 and 84 in 1983. It was the original intention to buy 1,366 aircraft for the Navy/Marines inventory, to be delivered until 1992 (probably later, as the funding rates have fallen short of the original 1978 plan). VFA-125 was formed as the Navy development squadron at NAS Lemoore in November 1980 and by 1983 some 105 Hornets had been delivered to Navy and Marines units. Despite foreign sales to Canada, Australia and Spain the rise in price has been so large that an F/A-18A is now more expensive than the larger and generally more capable F-14C (the price of which was the reason for developing the Hornet in the first place). In 1982 the Navy Secretary drew attention to this and threatened to delete all F-18 procurement after Fiscal 1983, buying instead further F-14 and A-6 aircraft (which were to be kept in production anyway). It is unlikely that the F-18 programme will be terminated at this early date, but its cost troubles are symptomatic of those afflicting most modern weapon systems.

McDonnell Douglas KC-10 Extender

KC-10A

Origin: Douglas Aircraft Company, Long Beach, California.
Type: Air-refuelling tanker and heavy cargo transport.
Powerplant: Three 52,500lb (23,814kg) thrust General Electric F103 (CF6-50C2) turbofans.
Dimensions: Span 165ft 4.4in (50.41m); length 181ft 7in (55.35m); height 58ft 1in (17.7m); wing area 3,958sq ft (367.7m²).
Weights: Empty (tanker role) 240,026lb (108,874kg); maximum loaded 590,000lb (267,620kg).
Performance: Maximum speed (max weight, tanker) about 600mph (966km/h) at 25,000ft (7,620m), maximum cruising speed, 555mph (893km/h) at 30,000ft (9,144m); takeoff field length, 10,400ft (3,170m); maximum range with maximum cargo load, 4,370 miles (7,032km); maximum range with max internal fuel, 11,500 miles (18,507km); landing speed at max landing weight, 171mph (275km/h).
Armament: None.
History: First flight (DC-10) 29 August 1970, (KC-10A) 12 July 1980.

Development: During the early 1970s the Air Force studied available commercial wide-body transports as a possible ATCA (Advanced Tanker/ Cargo Aircraft), and on 19 December 1977 announced the choice of a special version of the DC-10-30CF. The need had been highlighted by the difficulty of airlifting and air-fuelling USAF air units to the Middle East during the 1973 war, when some countries refused the USAF refuelling rights and the KC-135 and supporting cargo force found mission planning extremely difficult. The ATCA was bought to fly global missions not only with several times the overall payload of the KC-135, to a maximum of 169,409lb (76,842kg), but with the ability to provide tanker support to combat units whilst simultaneously carrying spares and support personnel. Compared with the DC-10-30 the KC-10A has a windowless main cabin, with large freight door and five passenger doors, a McDD high-speed boom with fly-by-wire control and able to transfer fuel at 1,500 US gal (5,678lit)/min, and a completely redesigned lower lobe to the fuselage housing seven Goodyear rubberized fabric fuel cells with capacity of about 18,125 US gal (68,610lit). Together with its own fuel the KC-10A has the ability to transfer 200,000lb

Above: Refuelling an F-15 Eagle from the 49th TFW affords a startling indication of the size of the KC-10A; another F-15 waits much nearer the camera. The Extender not only has a new design of boom but also a hose-drum unit and drogue alongside.

(90,718kg) to receiver aircraft at a distance of 2,200 miles (3,540km) from home base, and accompany the refuelled aircraft to destination. The cargo floor has improved power rollers and portable winch handling systems, and can accommodate 27 standard USAF Type 463L pallets.

The Air Force hopes eventually to be able to fund 36 KC-10A Extenders, though only at a low rate. In FY79 two aircraft were bought ($148 million, including some engineering costs), in FY80 a total of four, and in FY81 six. The second aircraft (79-0434) was the first to be delivered, to SAC at Braksdale AFB, Louisiana, on 17 March 1981. By July 1983 a total of 16 Extenders had been delivered, and, while commercial DC-10 production has been completed, the KC-10A line is likely to be kept open throughout the decade to a planned total force of 60 aircraft.

McDonnell Douglas/BAe
T-45 Hawk

T-45A and B

Origin: McDonnell Douglas, Long Beach, USA; British Aerospace is principal subcontractor.

Type: Advanced pilot trainer.

Engine: One 5,340lb (2,422kg) Rolls-Royce/Turboméca Adour 851 turbofan.

Dimensions: Span 30ft 9¾in (9.39m); length 36ft 7¾in (11.17m); height 13ft 3in (4.04m); wing area 179.6sq ft (16.69m²).

Weights: Empty (A) approx 8,756lb (3,972kg); loaded (clean) 12,440lb (5,642kg).

Performance: Maximum speed 645mph (1,038km/h); dive Mach limit 1.2; max rate of climb (gross wt) 9,300ft (2,835m)/min; service ceiling 50,000ft (15.24km); sortie endurance 4h.

Armament: Has full Hawk capability but no requirement for weapons at present.

History: First flight (Hawk) 21 August 1974, (T-45B) 1987, (A) 1988.

Above: ZA101 was the British Aerospace Hawk demonstrator which confirmed the selection of the type as the basis for the T-45.

Below: On the ground the VT/XTS demonstrator shows several differences from the T-45, including nose gear and airbrakes.

Development: Having had perhaps the quickest and most troublefree development of any modern military aircraft, the basic Hawk T.1 for the RAF entered service as a replacement for the Hunter and Gnat in 1976 and has subsequently set the world's best-ever record for any jet combat aircraft for low maintenance burden and low attrition (in the first 130,000 hours one aircraft was lost, through collision with a ship). In November 1981 a proposal by McDonnell Douglas, British Aerospace and Sperry Flight Systems was outright winner of the US Navy VT/XTS contest for a future undergraduate pilot trainer to replace the T-2C Buckeye and TA-4J Skyhawk. The three companies proposed a total system, of which aircraft and direct support represented some 85 per cent by value. Despite Congressional opposition the win was so clear-cut that it has been allowed to go ahead, and the first FSD (full-scale development) contact was signed in September 1982. The first stage involves delivery of 54 T-45B Hawk trainers from 1987 for land-based training. These are basically similar to the Hawk T.1 but have a strengthened landing gear with long-stroke main legs and twin-wheel nose gear, a modified rear fuselage with twin lateral airbrakes and revised cockpit instrumentation and avionics. From 1988 these would be supplemented by the T-45A, of which 253 are to be delivered, which in addition will have a nose-tow catapult facility and arrester hook. Though the fuel savings over today's aircraft are calculated at 35 to 55 per cent, the T-45A is not scheduled to enter service until 1991.

Northrop F-5

F-5A Freedom Fighter, F-5B, F-5E Tiger II, F-5F

Origin: Northrop Corporation, Hawthorne, California.
Type: Light tactical fighter.
Powerplant: Two General Electric J85 afterburning turbojets, (A/B) 4,080lb (1,850kg) thrust J85-13 or -13A, (E/F) 5,000lb (2,270kg) thrust -21A.
Dimensions: Span (A/B) 25ft 3in (7.7m) (A/B over tip tanks) 25ft 10in (7.87m), (E/F) 26ft 8in (8.13m), (E/F over AAMs) 27ft 11in (8.53m); length (A) 47ft 2in (14.38m), (B) 46ft 4in (14.12m), (E) 48ft 2in (14.68m), (F) 51ft 7in (15.72m); wing area (A/B) 170sq ft (15.79m²), (E/F) 186sq ft (17.3m²).
Weights: Empty (A) 8,085lb (3,667kg), (B) 8,36lb (3,792kg), (E) 9,683lb (4,392kg), (F) 10,567lb (4,793kg); max loaded (A) 20,576lb (9,333kg), (B) 20,116lb (9,124kg), (E) 24,676lb (11,193kg), (F) 25,225lb (11,442kg).
Performance: Maximum speed at 36,000ft (11km), (A) 925mph (1,489km/h, Mach 1.4), (B) 886mph (1,425km/h, Mach 1.34), (E) 1,077mph (1,734km/h, Mach 1.63), (F) 1,011mph (1,628km/h, Mach 1.53); typical cruising speed 562mph (904km/h, Mach 0.85); initial climb (A/B) 28,700ft (8,750m)/min, (E) 34,500ft (10,516m)/min, (F) 32,890ft (1,025m)/min; service ceiling (all) about 51,000ft (15.54km); combat radius with max weapon load and allowances, (A, hi-lo-hi) 215 miles (346km), (E, lo-lo-lo) 138 miles (222km); range with max fuel (all hi, tanks dropped, with reserves) (A) 1,565 miles (2,518km), (E) 1,779 miles (2,863km).
Armament: (A/B) total military load 6,200lb (2,812kg) including two 20mm M-39 guns and wide variety of underwing stores, plus AIM-9 AAMs

Above: An F-5E of the USAF Fighter Weapons School (part of the 57th Fighter Weapons Wing) at Nellis, in an Aggressors scheme.

for air combat; (E/F) Very wide range of ordnance to total of 7,000lb (3,175kg) not including two (F-5F, one) M-39A2 guns each with 280 rounds and two AIM-9 missiles on tip rails.
History: First flight (XT-38) 10 April 1959, (N-156F) 30 July 1959, (F-5A) 19 May 1964, (F-5E) 11 August 1972, (F-5F) 25 September 1974.
Development: The Air Force showed almost no interest in Northrop's N-156C Freedom Fighter, which was built with company funds and rolled out in

Northrop T-38 Talon

T-38A

Origin: Northrop Corporation, Hawthorne, California.
Type: Advanced trainer.
Powerplant: Two 3,850lb (1,746kg) thrust Genral Electric J85-5A afterburning turbojets.
Dimensions: Span 25ft 3in (7.7m); length 46ft 4½in (14.1m); wing area 170sq ft (15.79m²).
Weights: Empty 7,200lb (3,266kg); loaded 11,820lb (5,361kg).
Performance: Maximum speed, 858mph (1,381km/h, Mach 1.3) at 36,000 (11km); maximum cruising speed, 627mph (1,009km/h) at same height; initial climb 33,600ft (10.24km)/min; service ceiling 53,600ft (16.34km); range (max fuel, 20min loiter at 10,000ft/3km), 1,140 miles (1,835km).
Armament: None.
History: First flight (YT-38) 10 April 1959, (T-38A) May 1960; service delivery 17 March 1961.

Development: Throughout the second half of the 1950s Northrop's project team under Welko Gasich studied advanced lightweight fighters of novel design for land and carrier operation, but the first genuine service interest was in the N-156T trainer, a contract for Air Force prototypes being signed in December 1956. Unique in the world, except for the Japanese FST-2, in being designed from the outset as a jet basic trainer with supersonic speed on the level, the T-38 was an attractive lightweight version

Above: Popularly known as the White Rocket, the T-38A has been the standard graduation pilot trainer of the USAF since 1961. The type was replaced in the Thunderbirds team by the F-16A.

Rockwell OV-10 Bronco

OV-10A

Origin: Rockwell International, designed and built at Columbus, Ohio, Division of North American Aircraft Operations (now Columbus plant of NAA Division).
Type: Forward air control.
Powerplant: Two 715ehp Garrett T76-416/417 turboprops.
Dimensions: Span 40ft 0in (12.19m); length 41ft 7in (12.67m); wing area 291sq ft (27.03m²).
Weights: Empty 6,893lb (3,127kg); loaded 9,908lb (4,494kg), overload 14,444lb (6,552kg).
Performance: Maximum speed (sea level, clean) 281mph (452km/h); initial climb (normal weight), 2,600ft (790m)/min; service ceiling, 24,000ft (7,315m); takeoff run (normal weight) 740ft (226m); landing run, same; combat radius (max weapon load, low level, no loiter), 228 miles (367km); ferry range, 1,382 miles (2,224km).
Armament: Carried on five external attachments, one on centreline rated at 1,200lb (544kg) and four rated at 600lb (272kg) on short body sponsons which also house four 7.62mm M60 machine guns with 500 rounds each.
History: First flight 16 July 1965, (production OV-10A) 6 August 1967; USAF combat duty, June 1968.

Development: This unique warplane was the chief tangible outcome of prolonged DoD studies in 1959-65 of Co-In (Counter-Insurgency) aircraft tailored to the unanticipated needs of so-called brushfire wars using limited weapons in rough terrain. The Marines issued a LARA (Light Armed Recon Aircraft) specification, which was won by NAA's NA-300 in August 1964.

1959 without US markings. Eventually Northrop secured orders for over 1,000 F-5A and B fighters for foreign customers, and 12 of the MAP (Mutual Assistance Program) F-5As were evaluated by the Air Force in Vietnam in a project called Skoshi Tiger, which demonstrated the rather limited capability of this light tactical machine, as well as its economy and strong pilot appeal. When the USAF withdrew from SE Asia it left behind many F-5As and Bs, most having been formally transferred to South Vietnam, and few of these remain in the inventory. In contrast the slightly more powerful and generally updated F-5E Tiger II succeeded in winning Air Force support from the start, and the training of foreign recipients was handled mainly by TAC, with ATC assistance. The first service delivery of this version was to TAC's 425th TFS in April 1973. This unit at Williams AFB, Arizona (a detached part of the 58th TTW at Luke), proved the training and combat procedures and also later introduced the longer F which retains both the fire-control system and most fuselage fuel despite the second seat. Ultimately the Air Force bought 112 F-5Es, both as tactical fighters and (over half the total) as Aggressor aircraft simulating potential enemy aircraft in DACT (Dissimilar Air Combat Training). About 60 F-5Es and a small number of Fs continue in Air Force service in the development of air-combat techniques, in Aggressor roles, in the monitoring of fighter weapons meets and various hack duties. The F-5Es are painted in at least eight different color schemes, three of which reproduce Warsaw Pact camouflage schemes while others are low-visibility schemes. The F-5Fs at Williams are silver, with broad yellow bands and vertical tails. User units include the 58th TTW (425th TFS, as described), 57th TTW at Nellis (a major tactical and air combat centre for the entire Air Force), 3rd TFW, Clark AFB, Philippines (Pacaf), 527th Aggressor TFS, attached to the 10th TRW at RAF Alconbury, England, and various Systems Command establishments. In addition eight F-5Es are used by the Navy for Top Gun fighter-pilot training at the Naval Fighter Weapons School at NAS Miramar, California.

Above: Loaded only with data-link instrumentation probes, these four "Aggressors" F-5Es from the 527th Tactical Fighter Squadron at RAF Alconbury show all four current colour schemes.

of contemporary fighters, with twin afterburning engines, extremely small sharp-edged wings, area fuling for reduced transonic drag, inboard powered ailerons and slab tailplanes with slight anhedral. The instructor is seated behind and 10in (0.25m) higher than his pupil, both having rocket-assisted seats. To assist the pilot, yaw and pitch flight-control channels incorporate stability augmenters, and great care was taken in 1959-61 to produce an aircraft that pupils could handle. Strictly classed as a basic pilot trainer, the T-38A nevertheless is an advanced machine to which undergraduate pilots come only after completing their weed-out on the T-41A and their complete piloting course on the T-37A jet. The Air Force procured about 1,114 Talons, of which some 800 remain in inventory service with ATC. Their accident rate of some 0.9/11,2 per 1000,000 flight hours is half that for the USAF as a

whole An Advanced Squadron of T-38As is based at each ATC school (see Cessna T-37 for list). Many Talons are used as hacks by senior officers, for command liaison and for research, while others are assigned to TAC's 479th TTW at Holloman.

Below: This T-38A serves with TAC's 479th Tactical Training Wing at Holloman AFB (note WarPac number on nose), which also uses the AT-38B attack trainer.

Features included superb all-round view for the pilot and observer seated in tandem ejection seats, STOL rough-strip performance and a rear cargo compartment usable by five paratroops or two casualties plus attendant. Of the initial batch of 271 the Air Force took 157 for use in the FAC role, deploying them immediately in Vietnam. Their ability to respond immediately with light fire against surface targets proved very valuable, and the OV-10 was always popular and a delight to fly. In 1970 LTV Electrosystems modified 11 for night-FAC duty with sensors for detecting surface targets and directing accompanying attack aircraft, but most OV-10s now in use are of the original model. Units include TAC's 1st SOW at Hurlburt Field, Florida; the 602nd TACW, Bergstrom AFB, Texas; the 601st TCW, Sembach AB, Germany; Pacaf's 51st CW, Osan, Korea; and certain specialized schools. The Marine Corps received 114 OV-10As to a standard differing only in detail (such as radio equipment) from the USAF model. They have served with various VMO (observation) squadrons, duties including helicopter escort, FAC and armed recon. Since 1978 Rockwell has converted 17 to OV-10D standard for the NOS (night observation surveillance) role with a FLIR (forward-looking infra-red) and laser designator in a nose ball turret and an M97 three-barrel 20mm gun in a chin turret which can be slaved to the ball sensors.

Left: Carrying a 150-US gallon (568-liter) drop tank, this OV-10A was photographed on a training mission with the 51st Composite Wing from Osan AB in South Korea. In mid-1983 these aircraft were expected to be transferred to replace the light Cessna O-2A aircraft at Wheeler AFB, Hawaii. In turn they were to be replaced at Osan by the Cessna OA-37B, the A-37B reconfigured for FAC and observation duties on withdrawal from AFRES service. There is no move to fit the NOS systems to USAF OV-10s.

Rockwell B-1

B-1A, B

Origin: Rockwell International, North American Aircraft Operations, El Segundo, California.

Type: Strategic bomber and missile platform.

Powerplant: Four General Electric F101-GE-102 augmented turbofans each rated at 29,900lb (13,563kg) with full afterburner.
to 67° 30mins) 78ft 2½in (23.84m); length (including probe) 150ft 2½in

Dimensions: (B-1A) Span (fully spread) 136ft 8½in (41.67m), (fully swept, (45.78m); wing area (spread, gross) 1,950sq ft (181.2m²).

Weights: Empty (B-1A) about 145,000lb (65,772kg), (B) over 160,000lb (72,576kg); maximum loaded (A) 395,000lb (179,172kg), (B) 477,000lb (216,367kg).

Performance: Maximum speed (B, over 36,000ft/11km, clean), 825mph (1,328km/h, Mach 1.25); low penetration (B, clean) over 600mph (966km/h); high-alt cruising speed 620mph (1,000km/h); range (hi, unrefuelled) 7,455 miles (12,000km); field length, approx 4,500ft (1,372m).

Armament: Eight ALCM internal plus 14 external; 24 SRAM internal plus 14 external; 12 B28 or B43 internal plus 8/14 external; 24 B61 or B83 internal plus 14 external; 84 Mk 82 internal plus 44 (80,000lb, 36,288kg).

History: Original (AMSA) study 1962; contracts for engine and airframe 5 June 1970; first flight 23 December 1974; decision against production June 1977; termination of flight-test programme 30 April 1981; announcement of intention to produce for inventory, September 1981; planned IOC, 1 July 1987.

Above: The fourth B-1 prototype escorted in April 1981 by a chase F-111A. The B-1B will lack the long dorsal spine.

Development: Subject of a programme whose length in years far outstrips the genesis of any other aircraft, the B-1 was the final outcome of more than ten years of study to find a successor to the cancelled B-70 and RS-70 and subsonic in-service B-52. Originally planned as an extremely capable swing-wing aircraft with dash performance over Mach 2, the four prototypes were variable engine inlets and ejectable crew capsules of extremely advanced design. The latter feature was abandoned to save costs, and though the second aircraft reached Mach 2.22 in October 1978 this end of the speed spectrum steadily became of small importance. By 1978 the emphasis was totally on low-level penetration at subsonic speeds with protection deriving entirely from defensive electronics and so-called 'stealth' characteristics. Not very much could be done to reduce radar cross-section, but actual radar signature could be substantially modified, and the effort applied to research and development of bomber defensive electronic systems did not diminish.

The original B-1A featured a blended wing/body shape with the four engines in paired nacelles under the fixed inboard wing immediately outboard of the bogie main gears. Though designed more than ten years ago, the aerodynamics and structure of the B-1 remain highly competitive, and the extremely large and comprehensive defensive electronics systems (managed by AIL Division of Cutler-Hammer under the overall avionics integration of Boeing Aerospace) far surpassed those designed into any other known aircraft, and could not reasonably have been added as post-flight modifications. During prototype construction it was decided to save further costs by dropping the variable engine inlets, which were redesigned to be optimized at the high-subsonic cruise regime. Another problem, as with built with maximum wing sweep of 67° 30min. and were planned to have the B-52, was the increased length of the chosen ALCM, which meant that the original SRAM-size rotary launcher was no longer compatible. The original B-1 was designed with three tandem weapon bays, each able to house many free-fall bombs or one eight-round launcher. Provision was also made for external loads (see data). A particular feature was the LARC (Low-Altitude Ride Control), an active-control modification which by sensing vertical accelerations due to atmospheric gusts at low level and countering these by deflecting small foreplanes and the bottom rudder section greatly reduced fatigue of crew and airframe during low-level penetration. All four prototypes flew initially from Palmdale and exceeded planned qualities. The

Left: Close-up of the tail of the No 4 aircraft showing the lack of projections (except vortex generators) despite the avionics.

Sikorsky S-61 family

SH-3A and -3D Sea King, HH-3A, RH-3A and many other variants

Origin: Sikorsky Aircraft, Division of United Technologies.

Type: See text.

Engines: Two General Electric T58 free-turbine turboshaft; (SH-3A and derivatives) 1,250shp T58-8B; (SH-3D and derivatives) 1,400shp T58-10; (S-61R versions) 1,500hp T58-5.

Dimensions: Diameter of main rotor 62ft (18.9m); length overall 72ft 8in (22.15m); (61R) 73ft; height overall 16ft 10in (5.13m).

Weights: Empty (simple transport versions, typical) 9,763lb (4,428kg); (ASW, typical) 11,865lb (5,382kg); (armed CH-3E) 13,255lb (6,010kg); maximum loaded (ASW) about 18,626lb (8,449kg); (transport) usually 21,500lb (9,750kg); (CH-3E) 22,050lb (10,000kg).

Performance: Maximum speed (typical, maximum weight) 166mph (267km/h); initial climb (not vertical but maximum) varies from 2,200 to 1,310ft (670-400m)/min, depending on weight; service ceiling, typically 14,700ft (4,480m); range with maximum fuel, typically 625 miles (1,005km).

Armament: Very variable.

History: First flight 11 March 1959.

Above: A standard SH-3D anti-submarine helicopter from USS _Kitty Hawk_ with ASW Sqn HS-4 within Carrier Air Wing CVW-2.

Development: Representing a quantum jump in helicopter capability, the S-61 family soon became a staple product of Sikorsky Aircraft, founded in March 1923 by Igor Sikorsky who left Russia after the Revolution and settled in the United States. He flew the first wholly practical helicopter in 1940, and his R-4 was the first helicopter in the world put into mass production (in 1942). A development, the S-51, was in 1947 licensed to the British firm Westland Aircraft, starting collaboration reviewed on later pages. The S-55 and S-58 were made in great numbers in the 1950s for many civil and military purposes, both now flying with various turbine engines. The S-61 featured an amphibious hull, twin turbine engines located above the hull close to the drive gearbox and an advanced flight-control system.

First versions carried anti-submarine warfare (ASW) sensors and weapons, and were developed for the US Navy as the HSS-2, entering service in 1961-62 as the SH-3 series, with the name Sea King. By the early 1960s later variants were equipped for various transport duties, minesweeping, drone or spacecraft recovery (eg lifting astronauts from the sea), electronic surveillance and (S-61R series) transport/gunship and other combat duties. The S-61R family has a tricycle landing gear, the main wheels retracting forwards into sponsons and the cabin having a full-section rear loading ramp/door and a 2,000lb (907kg) roof-rail winch. The USAF model in this family was the CH-3E, 50 of which were rebuilt for combat operations with armour, self-sealing tanks, various weapons, rescue hoist and re-tractable flight-refuelling probe, and designated HH-3E Jolly Green Giant. The Coast Guard name for the HH-3F sea search version is Pelican. Total production of military models exceeded 770 by Sikorsky.

Above: The third prototype, with black radome, generally resembles a B-1B except for the spine, engine inlets and wing/engine fairings.

third was fitted with the ECM system and DBS (doppler beam-sharpening) of the main radar, while the fourth had complete offensive and defensive electronics and was almost a production B-1A. The Carter administration decided not to build the B-1 for the inventory, and the four aircraft were stored in flyable condition after completing 1,985.2h in 347 missions.

After further prolonged evaluation against stretched FB-111 proposals the Reagan administration decided in favour of a derived B-1B, and announced in September 1981 the intention to put 100 into the SAC inventory from 1986, with IOC the following year. The B-1B dispenses with further high-altitude dash features, the wing sweep being reduced to about

59° 30mins. As well as refined engines the B-1B can carry much more fuel; a detailed weight-reduction programme reduces empty weight, while gross weight is raised by over 37 tonnes. Main gears are stronger, wing gloves and engine inlets totally redesigned, many parts (ride-control fins, flaps and bomb doors, for example) made of composite material, pneumatic starters with cross-bleed fitted, offensive avionics completely updated (main radar is Westinghouse's APG-66), the ALQ-161 defensive avionics subsystem fitted, RAM (radar-absorbent material) fitted at some 85 loctions throughout the airframe, and the whole aircraft nuclear-hardened and given Multiplex wiring. Radar cross-section will be less than one-hundredth that of a B-52. Deploying this LRCA (Long-Range Combat Aircraft) is intended to bridge the gap until a next-generation 'stealth' aircraft can be fielded towards the end of the century.

Sikorsky S-64

S-64, CH-54A and B Tarhe

Origin: Sikorsky Aircraft Division of United Technologies, Stratford.
Type: Crane helicopter.
Engines: (CH-54A) two 4,500shp Pratt & Whitney T73-1 turboshafts, (CH-54B) two 4,800shp T73-700.
Dimensions: Diameter of six-blade main rotor 72ft 0in (21.95m); length overall (rotors turning) 88ft 6in (26.97m); height overall 18ft 7in (5.67m).
Weights: Empty (A) 19,234lb (8,724kg); maximum loaded (A) 42,000lb (19,050kg), (B) 47,000lb (21,318kg).
Performance: Maximum cruise 105mph (169km/h); hovering ceiling out of ground effect 6,900ft (2,100m); range with max fuel and 10 per cent reserve (typical) 230 miles (370km).
Armament: Normally none.
History: First flight (S-64) 9 May 1962; service delivery (CH-54A) late 1964, (B) late 1969.

Development: Developed from the first large US Army helicopter, the S-56, via the piston-engined S-60, the S-64 is an efficient weight-lifter which in Vietnam carried loads weighing up to 20,000lb (9,072kg). The CH-54A Tarhes used in that campaign retrieved more than 380 shot-down aircraft, saving an estimated $210 million, and carried special vans housing up to 87 combat-equipped troops. The improved CH-54B, distinguished externally by twin main wheels, has lifted loads up to 40,780lb (18,497kg) and reached a height of 36,122ft (11,010m). There is no fuselage, just a structural beam joining the tail rotor to the cockpit in which seats are provided for three pilots, one facing to the rear for manoeuvring with loads. The dynamic components (rotor, gearboxes, shafting) were used as the basis for those of the S-65. With cancellation of the HLH (Heavy-Lift Helicopter) the S-64 remains the only large crane helicopter in the West. A total of just over 100 were built, all the last batches being very small numbers for a late emerging civil market. By 1981 the CH-54 could be outperformed by the latest Chinook and Super Stallion, but its withdrawal from the USA is not scheduled until late in the decade.

Above: The CH-54A Tarhe has single mainwheels and one is seen here prior to installation of large inlet particle separators.

Sikorsky S-65

CH-53, HH-53 and RH-53 Sea Stallion, HH-53 Super Jolly (Green), CH-53E Super Stallion and export models

Origin: Sikorsky Aircraft, Division of United Technologies.
Type: See text.
Engines: (Early versions) two 2,850shp General Electric T64-6 free-turbine shaft; (CH-53D and G) 3,925shp T64 versions; (RH-53D) 4,380shp T64 versions; (CH-53E) three 4,380shp T64-415.
Dimensions: Diameter of main rotor (most, six blades) 72ft 3in (22.02m), (CH-53E, seven blades) 79ft 0in (24.08m); length overall (rotors turning) 88ft 3in (26.9m), (CH-53E, 99ft 1in, 30.2m); length of fuselage 67ft 2in (20.47m), (E, 73ft 4in, 22.35m); height overall 24ft 11in (7.6m), (E, 28ft 5in, 8.66m).
Weights: Empty (CH-53D) 23,485lb (10,653kg), (E) 32,878lb (14,913kg); maximum loaded (most) 42,000lb (19,050kg), (RH-53D) 50,000lb (22,680kg), (E) 73,500lb (33,339kg).
Performance: Maximum speed 196mph (315km/h); typical cruising speed 173mphj (278km/h); initial climb (most) 2,180ft (664m)/min, (E) 2,750ft (838m)/min; range (with payload, optimum cruise) (most) 540 miles (869km), (E) 1,290 miles (2,075km).
Armament: See text.
History: First flight 14 October 1964, (E) 1 March 1974; service delivery (CH-53A) May 1966, (E) March 1981.

Development: Obviously developed from the S-61, the S-65 family includes the largest and most powerful helicopters in production outside the Soviet Union. The dynamic parts (rotors, gearboxes and control system) were originally similar to those of the S-64 Skycrane family, but using titanium and with folding main-rotor blades. Most versions served in Vietnam from January 1967, performing countless tasks including recovery of downed aircraft. In 1968 a standard CH-53A completed a prolonged series of loops and rolls, while others set records for speed and payload. Most of the initial run of 139 CH-53As were for the Marine Corps, whose need for a heavy assault helicopter launched the programme in August 1962. A total of 15 were transferred to the Navy as RH-53A mine countermeasures (mine-sweeping) helicopters, and five to the USAF. Normal load is 38 troops, 24 stretchers and four attendants or 8,000lb (3,629kg) of cargo loaded through full section rear ramp/doors. To meet Vietnam needs the HH-53B Super Jolly was flown in March 1967, with a six-man crew, three Miniguns or cannon, armour, flight refuelling, extra fuel and rescue hoist. The CH-53C was a related transport version. The CH-53D had more power and auto-folding blades, with accommodation for 55 troops; 126 were built for the Marines in 1969-72 and most export versions are similar. The Navy took

Above: One of the original 5,700shp CH-53A assault transports of the US Marine Corps, which is now re-equipping with the 13,140shp CH-53E from which stems the Navy's MH-53E.

20 RH-53D, with long-range sponson/drop tanks and refuelling probe, and small numbers are being supplied toJapan. The HH-53H Super Jolly is a USAF rebuild of HH-53Cs with Pave Low night/all-weather search/rescue equipment including B-52 type inertial navigation, doppler, projected map display, AAQ-10 infra-red and APQ-158 terrain-following radar. The much-needed but costly CH-53E Super Stallion is virtually a different helicopter, selected in 1973 and finally ordered into production after costly delays (of political origin) in 1978. The rotor has seven blades, of greater length and titanium/glassfibre construction, the transmission rating is more than doubled in capacity to 13,140hp, the fuselage is longer and many other changes include a redesigned tail which, with the enlarged rotor, leans 20° to the left. The tailplanes were mounted low, but the production CH-53E has a kinked gull tailplane on the right. The first production machine flew on 13 December 1980 and funding began with six in 1978, 14 in 1979, 15 in 1980, 14 in 1981, 12 in 1982 and 11 in 1983, a total of 72. Deliveries by 1983 totalled 34. Total Navy requirement is put at 200, of which about two-thirds are for the Marines and 57 will comprise the MH-53E MCM (mine countermeasures) version. This has giant sponsons adding 1,000 US gal (3,785 litres) extra fuel and extremely complete minesweeping equipment; the first (the 35th aircraft modified) was to fly in September 1983.

Vought A-7 Corsair II

Vought A-7A to E, A-7K and TA-7C

Origin: Vought Systems Division of LTV, Dallas.
Type: Single-seat attack bomber (carrier- or land-based); (K, TA) dual trainer.
Engine: (A) one 11,350lb (5,150kg) thrust Pratt & Whitney TF30-6 two-shaft turbofan; (B, C) 12,200lb (5,534kg) TF30-8; (D) 14,250lb (6,465kg) Allison TF41-1 (Rolls-Royce Spey derivative) of same layout; (E) 15,000lb (6,804kg) TF41-2.
Dimensions: Span 38ft 9in (11.80m); length 46ft 1½in (14.06m); (TA) 48ft 2in (14.68m); height 16ft 0¾in (4.90m); (TA) 16ft 5in.
Weights: Empty (A) 15,904lb (7,214kg); (D) 19,781lb (8,972kg); maximum loaded (A) 32,500lb (14,750kg); (D) 42,000lb (19,050kg).
Performance: Maximum speed (all single-seat versions, clean) 698mph (1,123km/h) at low level; climb and ceiling, not reported (seldom relevant); tactical radius with weapon load, typically 71 miles (1,150km); ferry range with four external tanks, typically 4,100 miles (6,600km).
Armament: (A, B) two 20mm Colt Mk 12 in nose; six wing and two fuselage pylons for weapon load of 15,000lb (6,804kg). (D, E) one 20mm M61 Vulcan cannon on left side of fuselage with 1,000-round drum; external load up to theoretical 20,000lb (9,072kg).
History: First flight 27 September 1965; service delivery October 1966; first flight of D, 26 September 1968.

Development: Though derived from the Crusader, the Corsair II is a totally different aircraft. By restricting performance to high subsonic speed, structure weight was reduced, range dramatically increased and weapon load multiplied by about 4. Development was outstandingly quick, as was production. Vought built 199 7-A, used in action in the Gulf of Tonkin on 3 December 1967, followed by 196 B models. The C designation was used for the first 67 E models which retained the TF30 engine. In 1966 the Corsair II was adopted by the US Air Force. Compared with the Navy aircraft the A-7D introduced a more powerful engine (derived from the Rolls-Royce Spey) with gas-turbine self-starting, a multi-barrel gun, and above all a totally revised avionic system for continuous solution of navigation problems and precision placement of free-fall weapons in all weather. The folding wings and arrester hook were retained, and other features include a strike camera, boom receptacle instead of a probe, boron carbide armour over cockpit and engine, and a McDonnell Douglas Escapac seat. Avionics have been further improved over the years, but the

Sikorsky S-70

S-70, UH-60A Black Hawk, EH-60 (SOTAS), SH-60B Seahawk and UH-60D Night Hawk

Origin: Sikorsky Aircraft, Division of United Technologies Corporation.
Type: (UH) combat assault transport, (EH) electronic warfare and target acquisition, (SH) ASW and anti-ship helicopter.
Engines: (UH, EH) two 1,560shp General Electric T700-700 free-turbine turboshafts, (SH) two 1,690shp T700-401 turboshafts.
Dimensions: Diameter of four-blade rotor 53ft 8in (16.36m); length overall (rotors turning) 64ft 10in (19.76m); length (rotors/tail folded) (UH) 41ft 4in (12.6m), (SH) 41ft 0½in (12.5m); height overall (UH) 16ft 10in (5.13m); (SH) 17ft 2in (5.23m).
Weights: Empty (UH) 10,624lb (4,819kg), (SH) 13,648lb (6,191kg); maximum loaded (UH) 20,250lb (9,185kg) (normal mission weight 16,260lb, 7,375kg), (SH) 21,488lb (9,926kg).
Performance: Maximum speed, 184mph (296km/h); cruising speed (UH) 167mph (269km/h), (SH) 155mph (249km/h); range at max wt, 30 min reserves, (UH) 373 miles (600km), (SH) about 500 miles (805km).
Armament: (UH) provision for two M60 LMGs firing from side of cabin, plus chaff/flare dispensers; (EH) electronic only; (SH) two Mk 46 torpedoes and alternative dropped stores, plus offensive avionics.
History: First flight (YUH) 17 October 1974, (production UH) October 1978, (SH) 12 December 1979; serivce delivery (UH) June 1979.

Development: The UH-60 was picked in December 1976 after four years of competition with Boeing Vertol for a UTTAS (utility tactical transport aircraft system) for the US Army. Designed to carry a squad of 11 equipped troops and a crew of three, the Black Hawk can have eight troop seats replaced by four litters (stretchers), and an 8,000lb (3,628kg) cargo load can be slung externally. The titanium/glassfibre/Nomex honeycomb rotor is electrically de-iced, as are the pilot windscreens, and equipment includes comprehensive navaids, communications and radar warning. Deliveries to the 101st Airborne Division took place in 1979-81, followed by a further block of 100 to the 82nd Division in 1981. The EH-60A is an ECM (electronic countermeasures) version with Quick Fix II (as used in the Bell EH-1H) radar warning augmentation, chaff/flare dispenser and infra-red jammer. The EH-60B SOTAS (stand-off target acquisition system) is a dedicated platform for detecting and classifying moving battlefield targets under all weather conditions, with a data terminal in the cabin fed from a large rotating surveillance radar aerial under the fuselage (the main wheels retracting to avoid it). The Navy SH-60B is the air-vehicle portion of the LAMPS III (light airborne multi-purpose system), for which IBM is prime contractor. Though using the S-70 airframe, it is a totally different helicopter with equipment for ASW (anti-submarine warfare), ASST (anti-ship

Above: Sikorsky SH-60B Seahawk.

Below: Sikorsky UH-60A Black Hawk.

surveillance and targeting), search/rescue, casevac and vertical replenishment at sea. An APS-124 radar is mounted in the forward fuselage, 25 pneumatic launch tubes for sonobuoys in the left fuselage side and an ASQ-81 towed MAD (magnetic anomaly detector) bird on the right side at the rear. The Navy has indicated a requirement for 204 of these large and costly machines for service aboard the latest destroyers and frigates. Orders totalled 18 by mid-1982, additional to prototypes, and deliveries were to begin in 1983. By 1983 S-70 type helicopters may also be on order for the USAF. From December 1982 this service was to receive an initial 11 Black Hawks designated UH-60D with winterization gear and rescue hoist. They were expected to be followed by 90 HH-60D Night Hawk combat SAR machines with terrain-following radar, forward-looking infra-red, extra fuel, rescue hoist, comprehensive protection features and armament of Miniguns and Stinger (MLMS) missiles.

APQ-126 radar has been retained, programmable to ten operating models, together with British HUD, inertial system, doppler radar, direct-view storage tube for radar or Walleye guidance, and central ASN-91 digital computer. For laser-guided weapons the Pave Penny installation is hung externally in a pod, but the ALR-46(V) digital radar warning system is hung internal. There is no internal jamming capability, however, and the usual ECM payload is an ALQ-101 or -119 hung in place of part of the bombload.

Production of the A-7D has long been completed, but Vought has recently also delivered 30 of a planned 42 tandem dual-control A-7K Corsairs with full weapons capability. It is planned that 16 will be assigned to the ANG's 162nd TFTG at Tucson, and a pair to each of the 11 ANG's 13 operational units equipped with the A-7D. These units are the 112th TFG, Pittsburgh, Pennsylvania; 114th TFG, Sioux Falls, Iowa; 121st TFW, Rickenbacker AFB, Ohio; 127th TFW, Selfridge AFB, Michigan; 132nd TFW, Des Moines, Iowa; 138th TFG, Tulsa, Oklahoma; 140th TFW, Buckley, Colorado; 150th TFG, Kirtland AFB, New Mexico; 156th TFG, San Juan, Puerto Rico; 162nd TFG (TFG), Tucson; 169th TFG, McEntire Field, S. Carolina; 178th TFG, Springfield, Ohio; and the 185th TFG, Sioux City, Iowa. In the 1981 Gunsmoke tactical gunnery meet at Nellis the 140th, from Colorado, shot their way to the top team title with an exceptional 8,800 out of 10,000 points (the team chief, Lt-Col Wayne Schultz, winning the Top Gun individual award). The meet involves not only gunnery but bombing and maintenance/loaded contests. The chief of the judges said: 'Some of the scores are phenomenal—pilots are so accurate they don't need high explosive to destroy a target, they are hitting within 1½ to 2 metres, with ordinary free-fall bombs.' Few tactical aircraft are as good at attack on surface targets.

Apart from the A-7K the last model remaining in production for US service use was the ultimate Navy model, the A-7E. First flown as early as November 1968, this has an even more powerful TF41 than the USAF versions, but were otherwise very similar, with almost the same nav/attack systems, the only other major difference being replacement of the dorsal boom receptacle by a retractable probe. The E has been intensively used from the start, and the last of 596 was delivered in March 1981. From 1978 equipment included a FLIR (forward-looking infra-red) pod under the right wing and Marconi raster-HUD display for improved night and bad weather capability. It is not expected that the whole force will be thus equipped though 231 installations have been produced.

Left: Snakeye retarded bombs drop and fall smartly astern of an A-7D Corsair II of the USAF 23rd Tactical Fighter Wing at England AFB, Louisiana. This wing is one of those which has been re-equipped with the A-10A Thunderbolt II.